HR Resume Secrets

Secrets

**How To Create An Irresistible
Human Resources Resume That Will
OPEN DOORS, WOW HIRING MANAGERS
& GET YOU INTERVIEWS!**

Alan Collins

Success in HR Publishing
Chicago, Illinois USA

— CONTENTS —

HR Career Success Resources
by Alan Collins

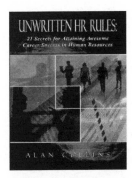

UNWRITTEN HR RULES:
21 Secrets for Attaining
Awesome Career Success
in Human Resources
Download Two Free Chapters
Available now at:
www.UnwrittenHRRules.com

BEST KEPT HR SECRETS:
400 Most Powerful Tips For Thriv-
ing At Work, Making Yourself
Indispensable & Attaining Outra-
geous Success in Human Resources
Download Free Excerpts
Available now at:
www.BestKeptHRSecrets.com

START YOUR OWN AWESOME
HR BLOG: The Absolute Beginner's
Guide To Launching Your Own
Human Resources Blog... Step-by-
Step, Quickly & From Scratch
Download One Free Chapter
Available now at:
www.AwesomeHRBlog.com

More HR Career Success Resources
By Alan Collins

WHY YOU NEED AN HR RESUME!

HOW TO USE THIS BOOK TO CREATE ONE THAT'S IRRESISTIBLE TO HIRING MANAGERS!

If you're a Human Resources professional, your resume is the most financially important document you will ever create. It is the FIRST thing anyone will ask you for before they'll agree to interview you.

So you absolutely must have one if you want to open doors and connect with hiring authorities. And you need one that powerfully differentiates YOU from...*and above*...the rest of the pack if you want to advance your career in today's highly competitive HR marketplace.

In fact, if you've NOT been getting interviews, chances are the way you've structured and used your resume is a big part of your problem.

However, the solution to that problem is now in your hands. *HR Resume Secrets* shows you step-by-step how to quickly and easily create a winning Human Resources resume -- and then use it to land those interviews.

At some point in your career, you'll need a resume. And the guidance within these pages will help you develop one NOW if:

- You've been laid off, want to change jobs, get promoted or you're in the job market for the first time.

1

- You've been networking like crazy, but you've had no interviews and you're feeling angry and frustrated.
- You're getting absolutely no response back from hiring authorities after submitting your credentials.
- You're not sure if your resume is a well-written, attention-getter that can truly elevate you from the rest of the crowded group also applying for the HR positions you want.
- You're confused about how to get your resume in the right hands in this era of online recruiting, keywords searches, applicant tracking systems, social media and new technology that do nothing but shield you from the real decision-makers.
- You're a busy and overworked HR professional who wants to act fast, doesn't want to learn useless theory or create a resume completely from scratch.

With all that said, let me deal right upfront with a question that might be rolling around in head at this point. And that is…

ARE YOU SERIOUS? DO I REALLY NEED A RESUME TO LAND A JOB IN HUMAN RESOURCES?

Resumes are dead, some people in HR will tell you. They're a waste of time these days. Don't create one. Never send one.

To them, I say: You're 100% wrong! Nothing could be further from the truth. You absolutely must have an HR resume and here's why:

Reason #1: There's unprecedented, intense competition for Human Resources positions at all levels. Today's corporate restructurings never end. Downsizings and job eliminations are a way of life in HR. As a result, many highly-qualified HR professionals and executives are always on the street seeking out opportunities. They're your competition.

And if you want to land a terrific HR position at any level, you need to more than ever set yourself apart from all these top notch contenders for the specific job you want. And the best way to do that lies in having a resume that can compellingly sell your best qualifications.

Let me put it another way. Envision yourself as a can of Pepsi. You know that you have lots of competition from Coke, Royal Crown Cola, Member's Mark Cola and other cola products. Your features include being brown, bubbly, cold, yummy and sweet; in a bottle or can; with added caffeine; and valued at about the same price. Your selling points include being refreshing, thirst quenching, energizing, satisfying, convenient and so on.

But here's the problem. *The other cola products can say the EXACT SAME THING!*

So what does Pepsi Cola do to differentiate itself in the marketplace? It's simple. *They advertise.* And the better, more compelling their advertising is, the more people will buy their product.

The same goes for you. Like Pepsi, you're a brand too. Except YOU are the product and your resume is your ad – and the latter needs to answer the question: "Why should we interview you?" Like a beautifully crafted advertisement, it should magnetically attract the reader, create a picture of a top performer and make you stand out from your competition, including those who may appear *more* qualified than you.

Reason #2: The old rules don't work anymore. The most successful strategies for the landing HR interviews today are different. You can no longer take out a piece of paper, slap together a quick list of your past jobs, write out what you've done, tout your education, describe yourself a "strategic business partner"…call that a resume…do some networking…and then wait to be buried with interview requests.

Ain't gonna happen. Sorry.

I'm sure you've looked at horrible HR resumes before. And you know as well as I do, that doing a half-assed job presenting your qualifications isn't going to fly anymore (if it ever did). Hiring authorities and interviewers today are too savvy. They

want to see a resume that looks compelling and sells you persuasively. And, that requires more prep work, better writing, and a
more eye-catching presentation if you want to convince them
that you are worthy of their time for a phone call or face-to-face
meeting.

If that wasn't challenging enough, in our high tech age, your
resume needs to be scannable, e-mailable, electronic, and readable on applicant tracking systems, visible on mobile devices or
available online at sites like LinkedIn so that it can be accessed
in the exact form that recruiters and hiring authorities want and
can work with. If it isn't, then your resume will disappear into
resume databases with thousands of others...and you will never
be found or heard from again.

So resumes are NOT dead. The rules are just different. You
need a resume more than ever. Just one that can make you stand
out from stronger competition, highlight your special strengths,
position you as the person they're looking for and presented in a
format preferred by recruiters, hiring authorities and those in
your network. And that's precisely what the information
throughout these pages will help you accomplish. That said...

HERE'S HOW TO QUICKLY SQUEEZE
THE MOST JUICE FROM THIS BOOK

**#1: Take 30 minutes to speed scan through the Chapters,
tips and strategies in this book.** The key points are bolded and
highlighted to jump off the page with the most important ideas.
Underline, jot notes and prioritize those strategies that you'll
want to apply first. If you use 25% of what's in this book,
you'll be ahead of the game. If you use 50% or more, you'll be
golden.

**#2: Go right to Chapter 11, find 2-3 resumes from the ex-
amples and use them to guide you as you prepare yours.**
There's no need for you to struggle or start from scratch! Use
these samples to provide a jolt of inspiration. You should be
able to locate a resume (or some combination of two, three or

more) that works for you. So take some time to review them. *For your added convenience, there is also a link where you can print out 8½ x 11" versions of all of them.*

#3: Download the free pre-formatted resume templates from the link in Chapter 12. I've saved you hours of time and money by putting together SEVEN "ready-to-go" templates that you're free to use to give you a running start. You can consume hours trying to get your resume spacing, fonts and formatting right. And that's time better spent focusing on your resume's content and doing networking. So go grab those resume templates, now. I'm sure there's at least one you'll want to use.

Finally, customize this book to your own situation. Everything written about here won't apply to you. So highlight those key sentences and chapters that do. Mark up the pages with your own notes. Make this book yours. Those of you who have read my previous books know that I like to keep things simple and this book will be no different. You'll find the concepts described here practical and easy to put into action.

Thank you in advance for investing your time in this book. I'm confident your returns will be massive.

Enjoy and best regards,

Alan Collins

Alan Collins

1

10 HUGE MISTAKES THAT PREVENT YOUR HR RESUME FROM PRODUCING LOTS OF INTERVIEWS FOR YOU

No matter how perfect a candidate you are, there are 10 major resume-related mistakes most HR professionals make that will sabotage your chances of landing interviews. You need to be aware of these <u>BEFORE</u> you start creating yours. Here they are:

Huge Mistake #1:
USING JUST ONE RESUME

Long gone are the days of having a single resume that you can use in all job situations. Or a single document that you can email blast to a thousand organizations at once.

Owning and using just one generic HR resume is old school. And it's like playing the lottery hoping you hit the jackpot. Sure, it's possible that your number will come up or that there's a direct match of your resume to a job -- but the chances of that happening is next to zero.

Today, more than ever, it is critical that your resume fit the specific job you are applying for. According to *Career Builder*,

97.4% of the resumes reviewed by recruiters, hiring managers and HR professionals don't match the requirements of the jobs those applicants are seeking. And experienced resume reviewers know this instantly. They've developed a sixth sense, based on all the resumes they've seen in the past, which enable them immediately tell if yours isn't a fit. If it's not, it's then either filed or trashed. In either case, that's not good news for you.

The point is that you must be prepared to change your resume and have different versions of it so that it matches what hiring authorities are looking for. In fact, let me take this one step further...

You should never apply for an HR job or give your resume to someone without first taking some time to ensure that you have <u>altered, tweaked or adapted it</u> -- so that it <u>fits the job</u> and <u>instantly positions you as a viable candidate for that position.</u> And the more precisely and specifically you can do this, the better.

Read that sentence again. Don't worry I'll wait. Yes, it's a mouthful and sounds daunting. However, in Chapter 3, I'll show you step-by-step exactly how to accomplish this. Just know for now that you MUST customize your resume for EVERY job.

Huge Mistake #2
NOT MAKING YOUR RESUME ROBOT-FRIENDLY

Have you ever applied online or at a company website for an HR job you thought you were absolutely perfect for, only to never hear back from the employer?

There's a very good reason why.

Chances are that your resume was kicked out of the application pool because you designed it for human eyes -- not for the robot eyes of Applicant Tracking Systems (ATS). ATSs are now used by most organizations to streamline the hiring process.

95% of large organizations (including almost all Fortune 500 companies) and 50% of mid-sized organizations employ them.

That's because the number of resumes most organizations receive is overwhelming. When I worked at PepsiCo, we received 90,000 resumes a month...and 14% of them were for Human Resources positions! And we were far from unique. Google recently reported that they get on average 75,000 resumes a week at their corporate headquarters. I would surmise nearly all large companies with 1,000 or more employees are buried up to their eyeballs in resumes.

Because of this huge volume, unless you're applying for a specific HR position, your resume is digitized and stored in an ATS data base with thousands of others. While stored, most systems will then do absolutely nothing with it unless it is specifically needed by a recruiter or a hiring manager. If there's no available and relevant job, it can sit in that data base for years and literally never be seen or read by an actual human being at any point during that time.

What makes this situation even worse is that, according to a LinkedIn study, only 15% of the people sending in resumes are *actually qualified* for the positions they're applying for. That means 85% of them are considered trash by hiring authorities, executive recruiters and resume screeners – which they are well aware of. And that's why companies welcome the help of the ATS technology to help them sift through the crap to identify the few jewels worthy of their time and effort.

If that wasn't bad enough, even when the position you want is open, your resume faces an additional hurdle. And that hurdle is called KEYWORDS. The ATS will analyze the words in your resume and compare them to the KEYWORDS of the position you want to determine if there's a match.

For example, for an HR role requiring collaborative labor relations experience, the important resume keywords could be: *interest-based bargaining, contract negotiations, grievances, labor relations, arbitration, chief spokesperson, 7 years of experience.*

Likewise, for an Organization Development Director's job working with Sales, the keywords they're looking for could be: *sales, organization development, program design, facilitation, leadership development, mentoring, succession planning, performance management, Masters degree, 7 years of experience.*

The more keywords on your resume that match, the better your chances are of getting a closer look (this time, with human eyes) and then possibly getting contacted.

Of course, zero or very few matched keywords mean your resume won't get a second read by the recruiter or hiring authority. And no second read means you're out of luck!

Here's the point: Your resume must not only be pleasing to human eyes, but it should also be robot-friendly for Applicant Tracking Systems which utilize keywords for screening. I'll explain more about how to successfully conquer these robots in Chapter 4.

Huge Mistake #3
USING THE WRONG RESUME STYLE

Style matters. And there is one particular resume style that many HR folks frequently use that greatly reduces their chances of getting interviewed. It's also the one wrongly recommended by many paid resume experts. And that is...

The Functional Resume.

They're a no-no. Don't use them.

To clarify, a functional resume focuses primarily on the *professional skills, competencies or accomplishments* you bring to a specific target job. In fact, these areas take up just about all the space on the resume. And in so doing, it accomplishes its real purpose...which is to *de-emphasize your previous job history, employers and employment dates* by placing them on the second page, which usually gets less attention than your lead page. To see an example of a functional resume, check out Thea Jones' document (her BEFORE version) in Chapter 11.

The philosophy behind this style of resume is that because the focus is on your skills and accomplishments (and not the context or time you acquired them), employers will be less interested in your job titles and previous employers.

This is fallacy.

Nevertheless, many resume consultants advise people to use a functional resume if they are reentering the workforce, leaving the military, pursuing a different job function, or are seeking their first job. In these cases, it is entirely possible that it might get read, but even then the odds are slim.

So, to be clear, I don't advise that you use a functional resume for these very specific reasons:

- **It looks like you're hiding something** -- either too many jobs, gaps in your work history or something else that a conventional resume format would expose. As a result, it conveys distrust and deception. The functional resume is almost never used by job seekers with perfect histories — and most savvy recruiters know that. When they get this style of resume from an applicant, a red flag goes up immediately that something's not right. So when they read the resume (*if* they read it) their focus is on trying to figure out what's wrong instead of what's right with the job seeker. Not good!

- **It's unclear when and where your achievements occurred.** Because your key accomplishments aren't linked to a specific position or company, it can sometimes feel like you're making wild, unsubstantiated claims. And even if there is a clue as to where an achievement took place, it has to be cross-checked with the Work History section to see *when* it happened. That's extra work and a pain in the butt. And most busy recruiters simply won't bother trying to connect the dots.

- **It doesn't fit well with Applicant Tracking Systems.** Functional resumes make keyword searches more complicated because the database system can't match up the keyword achievements with the dates because the functional format has them in entirely separate sections.

- **It's not conventional.** No matter what you read, most employers prefer the status quo and despise change. They want employees who fit smoothly into their company culture and conventions. Starting with your resume, it's important that you show that you fit in by using a more traditional resume — instead of one that's more functional.

- **It's a quick way to get weeded out.** Finally, with the volume of resumes hiring authorities receive, they're quickly looking for any reasons to drop yours. And most of the time they just toss functional resumes without any further review.

So, avoid this type of resume! There are simply too many risks and downsides. There's only ONE format I recommend and it is described in Chapter 2.

Huge Mistake #4
OVERUSING BUZZWORDS AND JARGON

The words you use to describe yourself on your resume are crucial. Loading it up with squishy, unspecific, meaningless statements like *"superb written and oral communication skills," "highly motivated,"* or *"great leader"* don't do you any favors.

LinkedIn recently did an analysis of the profiles of its 200 million users and came up with a list of the most overused words and expressions. Here are their top ten:

1. Extensive experience
2. Innovative
3. Motivated
4. Results-oriented
5. Dynamic
6. Proven track record
7. Team player
8. Fast-paced
9. Problem solver
10. Entrepreneurial

Over half of these apply to HR and validates what I've suspected for years, which is that certain overused words and phrases have no absolutely effect on executives or hiring managers. Using them just tells them that you're boring, forgettable or just like everyone else.

To avoid this, find unique ways to describe your brilliance. For example, as an alternative, try asking yourself: "When someone reads my resume, can the reader say without hesitation why I should matter to them?

If you're going to state your *"superb communications skills,"* or your *"outstanding leadership"* back up these statements with facts and examples.

In Chapter 7, I'll cover how to more powerfully sell your experience without resorting to empty statements and jargon.

Huge Mistake #5
OVERDOING CONFIDENTIALTY

Many folks assume that including the word *"Confidential"* on their resume keeps their information private. With this in mind, they will state *"Current Employer Confidential, 2013 - Present"* instead of naming the current company.

Don't fall in this trap.

Potential employers want to know upfront who you're working for -- especially if they have lots other resumes to choose among (and most times they do). With this information missing, yours likely won't get read.

Simply stated, any time you submit your resume to a prospective employer, you run the risk of your job search being discovered by your present employer. That's just the reality of today's job market. In fact, this has become even more complicated now that resumes are posted on literally thousands of online sites or job boards. So, no matter how confidential you try to be, if you're looking for a job while presently employed, you may be discovered. That's the risk.

If you are worried, and rightfully so, about confidentiality, then don't send your resume to specific hiring authorities

until after you've spoken with them on the phone – or unless you're about to lose your job and don't care if your present employer finds out. In any event, don't assume your search will be kept quiet and be careful where you send your resume.

Huge Mistake #6:
PROVIDING TOO MUCH INFORMATION

Clearly, you need to disclose your employment history. But, you've gone overboard if you're guilty of any of the following:

Submitting too many pages.
There you are, late one evening, rushing to update your resume so you can respond to a hot job opportunity. But the moment your fingers touch the keyboard, your brain serves up the question that bedevils every job seeker...*How long should your resume be? Should it be one page? Two pages? More?*

If you call up three of your HR colleagues, I guarantee you'll get three different answers. And if you query Google, it only gets worse. But you still need to send out that resume tonight, so the last thing you have time for is a philosophical debate. So what do you do? I'll share some resume rules of thumb with you in Chapter 4. Here's a tiny hint: don't send 10 pages.

Citing reasons for leaving jobs.
Years ago, I had a candidate who, after each job listed on his re- sume, included a description of why he had left that job. After three of such explanations, he wrote "Laid off due to downsiz- ing." I passed on him. There were too many other better candidates. I'm not alone. Hiring authorities look for reasons *not* to interview you as much as for reasons they *should*. So, there's no need to explain why you left any job on your resume. Wait for the interview to verbally answer that question.

Disclosing your current or desired earnings.
Don't *ever, ever* include your past, present, or desired earnings on your resume. This will automatically eliminate you from too

many opportunities. Even if it is required, think twice before divulging this information. Salary history and salary requirements are most often used to screen you out of consideration. Usually your salary is either too high *("we can't afford you")* or too low *("why aren't you worth more?")*. But relax, in Chapter 14, I'll share more details on how to respond to salary requests.

Sharing personal information.
As a general rule, I don't recommend including personal data, and the reason is simple. Deep down, when employers are screening resumes, they don't give a rip that you golf, bike, play the piano or collect antique furniture. And including certain information can actually work against you getting interviewed. For example, if you're a woman, married with three kids in grade school, an employer may secretly question your ability to travel 75% of the time if the HR job they're filling requires it.

Having said all this, there are exceptions to every rule. Employers who hire HR leaders want people, not robots. They want to know who you really are, whether you can fit in their corporate culture, and what makes you tick. As an example, I remember one candidate that included the following at the end of his resume:

> Purdue Alumni Association Board Member...Windy City Bike Club... Avid Golfer and Tournament Tennis Player... Brown Belt in Karate.

As a Purdue alum and biker myself, this candidate connected with me instantly on a variety of levels -- and having this on his resume kept me reading. However, the rest of his qualifications didn't match what we were looking for and I dropped him from the process. Darn!

The point is including personal information like this is a hit or miss proposition and a low-priority, "nice-to-have" item. It should ONLY be included if you know with <u>absolute certainty</u> that it would stimulate interest or help you establish a personal connection with your interviewers...and you have enough space to include it. Otherwise, forget it.

Stating that "References are available upon request."
Historically, this has been included at the bottom of resumes. However, it's unnecessary because:

- Employers just naturally assume you will provide this information, if asked.
- This statement takes up valuable white space that you can use to further sell your qualifications.
- Most employers won't take the time to check references until after an interview. By then, they will already have your completed application with a list of your references.

The bottom line:
Each word on your resume is sacred, so choose wisely. Every single phrase you use must serve a purpose. And that purpose is simple: to get the reader to read on. Look at it as a competition. For a word to be on the page, it needs to be one hell of a mighty word. The better you choose your words, the more likely they will help sell the reader on why you deserve to be interviewed.

Huge Mistake #7:
BELIEVING YOUR RESUME CAN
OVERCOME DIGITAL DIRT

It doesn't matter how terrific your resume is if you don't clean up your digital dirt.

What's digital dirt?

Let me explain with a story I first told on my blog.

I recently had coffee with an executive headhunter at one of Chicago's largest search firms.

She was doing a search for a Senior HR Director for a well-known oil company based in Texas. This job had the works. Great pay. Great benefits. Great location. An awesome future. This was the type of dream job HR folks with 7-10 years of experience would kill for.

Anyway, she came across an HR candidate whose resume looked outstanding. She then went online to check him out further after completing a quick phone exploratory chat with him. She reviewed his LinkedIn profile and then googled his name.

And, her jaw dropped! On his Facebook page, she found twelve pictures of this candidate half-naked at a friend's bachelor party. It included various sexually suggestive poses with exotic dancers. And, as she looked further down his page, he had numerous comments about his gambling habits, drinking, recreational drug use and nights out on the town.

"Holy crap!" she thought. At that point, she didn't care that this was his personal life. She didn't care that his Facebook privacy settings were probably not turned on. And, it didn't matter to her one bit that this candidate was clearly showing off online.

All that mattered to her was...

In five minutes, this candidate had gone from hero to zero! And he suddenly became someone who looked immature, unprofessional and a high risk hire.

AND IT DIDN'T MATTER HOW AWESOME HIS RESUME WAS!

She confessed that, while she's pretty open-minded herself, there wasn't a snowball's chance that she'd be presenting him to her client as a candidate for such a terrific HR job. As far as she was concerned, this HR dude was toast. Finished. History. There would be no follow-up or further interviews.

All because this candidate did not take steps to clean up his "digital dirt" and he allowed it to creep in and tarnish his online image and reputation.

The question we both asked ourselves as we sipped our coffee was: "What the heck was this guy thinking?"

But more importantly, what does this mean for you?

Why am I telling you this?

Here's why...

It is absolutely no secret that if you're an HR pro in the job market, you're going to get googled. Expect it.

In fact, research by ExecuNet revealed that 92% of recruiters reported using search engines to find background data on candidates before bringing them in for interviews.

Of that number, 35% eliminated a candidate because of what they found online. They're looking for the good, the bad, and the ugly on any website a quick search can turn up. That will include any presence you have on LinkedIn, Facebook, Twitter, YouTube, Squidoo and the like.

So, it doesn't matter if you're seeking an entry-level HR role or a senior executive position, someone is going to take five seconds and put your name through the Google machine in pursuit of digital dirt.

Now, you might say – great, google me. You're not going to find anything. And you know what…

That's even worse!

If you're checked out online and nothing shows up, what this means is that you probably don't have a web site…that you've probably have not given a speech to an prominent organization…that you've probably never written any HR articles…that you've probably never done any work of note in the community or with a charity…that you've probably never held a prominent role in a HR professional organization…that you've not doing anything that has distinguished you professionally within your company or anywhere else for that matter.

That's what it could mean when nothing shows up.

Now understand, none of that may be true.

But that's how you could be perceived by a recruiter or hiring manager.

Now, I know that's not fair. What's personal is personal.

But life ain't fair.

On the other hand, I've just reminded you of an important, game-changing tip for your success…and that is: *how to enhance your online image.*

Because of how important this is to your career, <u>don't wait</u> to read the rest of this book. Start cleaning up your image right now! How? By following these three steps:

Step 1: Google your name and assess what you find. If nothing significant shows up, capitalize on this opportunity to create from scratch an attractive online image and persona for yourself. This could include putting plans in place to:

- Get 8-10 of your contacts to add testimonials to your LinkedIn profile. This number of endorsements will blow hiring managers away and add immense credibility to your experience and credentials.
- Speak at an HR workshop, local SHRM meeting or a professional business society on an HR topic.
- Write articles and publish them online or on a blog.
- Involve yourself in the community -- such as spearheading a fundraiser for charity or becoming a spokesperson for the group's causes.
- Take on the leadership role in noteworthy public relations activities at your company.
- Or finally, create your own web site. A quick way to do this is to create a Look Up Page. You can find more details at LookUpPage.com. The information there will enable you to create a professional web page for yourself in just 5 minutes that guarantees your appearance on Google's first page when someone searches your name.

Step 2: If unflattering stuff about you DOES show up online, don't delay...take steps right now to get rid of it. Start by taking down damaging images or posts about you. If there are any current or "college days" photos on any of your websites that show you using alcohol, drugs, or posing with knives or guns in a threatening manner, these should be deleted immediately.

If you have potentially embarrassing photos or posts that are on a *friend or family member's website,* contact them and ask that the photos or posts be removed.

Also check to see if there are any photos or posts like this on your Facebook page or Twitter account.

If you have linked your Twitter page to another website, it's also possible for potential employers to see other questionable photos or posts at that site as well.

Have all this scum wiped clean. Period.

Step 3: If the digital dirt on you is really bad or difficult to remove, take even stronger action. Some online information about you may be tough to erase. For example, you might find your name in a lawsuit or find libelous comments that someone has written about you.

If that's the case, find out who is operating the website and ask that the information be taken down. If this doesn't get this stuff removed, then set up a blog to counter the accusations against you or contact a lawyer.

Depending on the severity of what you find about yourself online, and depending on whether you believe it could damage your career and future, you might need assistance from a professional. Besides a lawyer, you might also want to reach out to a public relations expert or an online reputation specialist.

One thing's for sure, paying attention to your online reputation is part of the career game these days.

You never know when someone will check you out online before an interview. (If you're single, do you Google someone before agreeing to go out a first date with them? I thought so!)

The best advice I can give is to simply avoid publishing potentially damaging or inappropriate content starting right now.

If you think that something you post online will negatively impact your ability to land a job now or even ten years from now, don't blog it, tweet it, put it in your Facebook profile or write about it anywhere.

It's not worth it.

So google-proof yourself.

Remove your digital dirt.

You never know who could be looking you up online at this very moment. It could be someone prepared to interview you for the HR job of your dreams. So act now!

With that said, let's move on to…

Huge Mistake #8:
USING GIMMICKS

Here are just a few examples of gimmick resumes I've received:

- A resume attached to a cereal box. (Submitted by a candidate for an HR manager's position at Quaker Oats).

- A bright green resume with the candidate's picture on it drinking Gatorade. (Obviously, someone hoping to stand out when applying for a Gatorade HR director's job).

- A resume contained in an egg carton with faux eggs with a message saying "I can deliver fresh candidates for you daily." (Thoughtfully provided by a candidate for a position in Staffing & Talent Acquisition).

- A resume packaged with a bunch of colored sticky stars that fell out when opened, along with a cover letter saying "HIRE A STAR" on top.

- A resume printed on a slightly oversized (20" x 24") poster board.

- An express mail box containing the candidate's resume along with a bottle of expensive wine and a gift certificate for dinner. This bribe…er, gift, though tempting, was returned. Sad, but true.

- Video resumes from numerous candidates. Out of curiosity, I viewed one once. Never again! I watched as the content of the actual resume crawled across the bottom of the screen at a frenzied pace. It was a stunning, high-tech visual presentation. But at the end of the video I realized that I had just wasted 5 minutes of a busy work day watching a movie. Meanwhile, I retained none of the applicant's pertinent information and there was no way for me to access the resume content in this video without committing to viewing it again or transcribing it. So I trashed it. (Sorry if you're reading this).

I could provide more examples, but hopefully you get the point. Some of these zany approaches will definitely attract attention. And in return, they will elicit a reaction -- positive or negative. However, if you don't know how the resume reviewer will react, why run the risk of rejection right off the bat?

As a rule of thumb, unless you're applying for position in Marketing or the company's most innovative division, most overly creative, offbeat resume tactics simply DON'T work. *This is Human Resources!* While a bizarre resume format may get you a few more seconds of eyeball time during the screening process, it will also prevent your resume from making it through electronic filtering tools used by the bigger corporations.

Recruiters prefer things that are familiar and make their jobs easier...not tougher. Most times, they aren't looking for the most creative HR candidate; they're simply looking for the best fit. So just give them what they want in EXACTLY the format they request -- concise and targeted to their needs.

The truth is if you've not been successful with your resume, you don't need a better gimmick, *you need a better résumé.* And that comes from focusing more on your "selling points" and less on tricks and games.

Huge Mistake #9
LYING, SPINNING OR MISREPRESENTING FACTS

In my 25+ years in HR, I personally know of eight professionals in our field that screwed themselves out of a job because they lied on their resumes. Here are three of them:

- **John covered up his last job as an HR Director by not including it on his resume**. He simply extended the employment dates for one of his other jobs and was counting on the difference not being discovered. However, when we did a post-hire reference check and the dates didn't match up, John confessed that he was fired after six months from the job he hid. And we fired him too, for lying.

- **Kristen "stretched reality" too much when she applied for a Senior Manager role in our Compensation & Benefits group.** On her resume, she claimed to have led a major company-wide redesign of the executive bonus program. This was a critical experience needed for the job she applied for. However, we discovered that she was, in fact, merely doing research supporting the redesign team...*wasn't even a member of that team*...and certainly NOT the leader of the project. Admittedly, this type of fabrication is tough to discover. And we only found this out when a member of our interview team told us she knew the *real* project leader -- and it wasn't Kristen! When we checked things out and confirmed that Kristen had indeed misrepresented her experience, we decided to move on to other candidates.

- **Carmen was less than truthful when she submitted her resume for a Talent Acquisition position.** She had tremendous experience working for a variety of staffing agencies and was a pro at using social media to source candidates. She also claimed to have received her B.S. degree from University of Miami. When the university couldn't validate her as a graduate...and she couldn't produce any evidence supporting her degree completion...we quickly rescinded our offer.

In this latter case, I've never quite understood why people will lie about having a degree. It's so easy to verify this information.

Even if you're seeking an HR role in a tiny organization with a limited budget, it's inexpensive to have your educational credentials checked. There are lots of online clearinghouses that perform this task for any firm for just a few dollars.

As a fellow HR professional, I don't want to insult your intelligence. I know I'm about to make some obvious points here. But they deserve to be reiterated. So here goes:

- **If you lie on your resume and it is discovered beforehand, you're NOT going to get called in for interviews or hired.**

- **If you lie and it is discovered *after* you are hired, there's a high probability you will get canned.**

Life's too short. It's not worth the hit to your reputation. So, don't spin, lie or misrepresent facts on your resume. Period. 'Nuff said. Let's move on to...

Huge Mistake #10
NOT PROOFREADING

ONE single, stinking resume error can instantly disqualify you. Don't believe me, here's the data:
- According to *Career Builder*, 61% percent of recruiters will automatically dismiss a resume because it contains typos.
- 43% percent of hiring managers will disqualify a candidate from consideration because of spelling errors (according to a study by *Adecco*).
- And the use of an unprofessional email address will get a resume rejected 76% of the time (*BeHiring.com*).

Spelling mistakes, grammatical errors, missing information, too much information and words that are out of place all contribute to increasing the chances of your resume being trashed.

Don't let this happen. Get proofing help. Before you even start writing your resume, line up 1-2 trusted HR colleagues in advance to review your resume. Pick some folks with your best interests at heart and good attention to detail. You want it flawless, so get an objective second opinion.

Making your resume pristine increases the chances of landing your HR dream job.

There you have it: the 10 biggest mistakes that HR professionals make in preparing their resumes that costs them interviews. Before you start crafting yours, make sure you have planned to take care of these miscues in advance.

THREE STRATEGIES
FOR GETTING YOUR RESUME
NOTICED, READ & ACTED UPON!

Strategy 1:
Use The One HR Resume Style
Employers Prefer Most

Strategy 2:
Create These Two Types of
Human Resources Resumes

Strategy 3:
Plan To Deliver Your HR Resume Three
Different Ways For Maximum Exposure
To Hiring Authorities

2

Strategy One:
USE THE ONE HR RESUME STYLE
EMPLOYERS PREFER MOST

It does you no good to create a fabulous resume if nobody reads, notices or acts on it. If you've ever angrily wondered: "What can I do to make my resume stand out, reach the desk of the hiring manager and get reviewed?," this chapter will lay out the first of three strategies that will begin to answer that question.

As you may recall in Chapter 1, we discussed the resume style that many HR folks have used unsuccessfully: namely the functional resume. Let's now reveal the one most preferred by hiring authorities. And it is...

The standard, reverse chronological style.

It is the ONE and ONLY style you should use. Don't let anyone talk you into doing anything different. All the example resumes in Chapter 11 utilize this style. And its basic framework is illustrated on the next page as Exhibit 2-1.

Just as its name implies, this style provides a reverse chronology—that is, a historical timeline—of your work experience. Its main feature is that it consolidates what you did, how well you did them with your employer and your employment dates.

Exhibit 2-1: Preferred Style – The Reverse-Chronological Resume

YOUR NAME
Your Address, City, State, Zip
Phone number, E-mail address

SUMMARY
[A summary of highlights that include the most important facts and appealing information located at the visual center of the page.]

EXPERIENCE
[Year] - Present, Name of Company
[Short explanation of what the company does or explanation of the division of a large company, so that anyone can clearly understand it.]

Job Title: [Make sure this title is commonly understood. If not, explain it in common terms. Also include a clear and specific explanation of your major responsibilities and the specific results you've attained. Write all the way from one margin to another so that you can get as much information on one page as possible. Write *no more* than a three- or four-sentence paragraph that a high school senior could understand.]

Name of Company [Same as above] *[Year] - [Year]*
Job Title: [Same as above. If your title is "odd," you may want to change it to make it resonate better: Just be sure to explain to an interviewing or hiring authority what you've done during the interview.]

- Remember, *numbers* and *statistics* pack power and punch, get recognized and paid attention to. So work hard to "quantify" what your successes and accomplishments have been.
- Percentage improvements in key HR metrics, cost savings, size of a department, even amounts of budgetary responsibility are noticed. Highlight or boldface any outstanding "numbers" that will set you apart from other candidates.

Name of Company [Same as above] *[Year] - [Year]*
Job Title: [Same as above]
The further back you go in your job history, the less you have to explain about what you did and how you did it. But of course you'll want to mention any outstanding accomplishments.

> ***How to Handle Previous Experience:*** If your experience goes back more than 15 years, leave it out entirely -- or summarize all of it in two or three sentences.

EDUCATION
[College or University, type of degree, beginning with the graduate degree first and year of graduation. If no degree was conferred, simply put the years of attendance. Any honors such as high grade point average should be noted. Any formal school less than college need not be included. Any continuing education (such as HR certifications, professional development or key leadership affiliations could be mentioned here.]

As we'll discuss later, there are slight variations to the reverse, chronological resume, but for the most part writing your
resume is that simple. And using this style provides you with a
number of advantages as a candidate:

**Advantage #1: Recruiters and hiring managers are very
comfortable with this resume style as it's the one most utilized throughout the world.** Most managers have a clear idea
of what they expect to see when they read a resume. And that's
a good thing. Reading one is a bit like walking into a restaurant—they know what to expect. In a restaurant, they know that
there will be tables and a menu, that they will be asked for their
order, and that they will have to pay for the food.

They might even expect to leave a tip.

All very familiar.

On the other hand, receiving an unusual resume would be like
walking into the restaurant and seeing no tables or serving staff.
They might figure out that there is a food vending machine to
use or they might just walk out confused. Similarly, when viewing your resume, they might persevere and read an unusual
resume, or he or she might simply reject it. Most will overwhelmingly choose the latter.

**Advantage #2: This style is also easily digested in applicant
tracking systems and won't raise suspicions that you're trying to hide professional skeletons...**such as a former conviction
as a serial job hopper. Instead it:

- Showcases a progression of increasingly responsible positions, especially preferred by executive recruiters and
  decision-making committees for management and top-
  tier executive slots.
- Demonstrates that you are qualified to take the next step
  in your career.
- Highlights impressive employers who will add weight to
  your credentials because of their name recognition, comprehensive training programs or strong market position.

- Answers the employer's questions about whether your work history has been stable.

The only pitfall to using this style of resume is that it really puts you under the microscope. It's like wearing skimpy swimsuit to the beach: If you're not in great shape, it will show every roll and dimple. Gaps in employment, lack of a strong career progression, and other potential negatives will be easily identified. And if that's the case, don't be overly concerned -- I'll share with you some strategies on how to overcome these issues in Chapter 13.

3

Strategy Two:
CREATE THESE TWO TYPES
OF HUMAN RESOURCES RESUMES

The second strategy for getting your resume noticed, read and acted upon involves creating two different types of resumes. They are the:
- Universal Resume
- Customized Resume

Each of them utilizes the reverse, chronological style we discussed in previous chapter. In this chapter, we'll detail how to prepare each of these documents and the situations in which you should use them. With that in mind, let's get started with...

Resume #1:
YOUR UNIVERSAL RESUME

This is your foundational, all-purpose resume. It serves as your master document. It's a template from which you'll create more customized, job-targeted resumes. It includes the best possible summary of your experiences, skills, dates, layout, and chronology.

To develop it, think about a job you can nail. That is, a job you can make the most convincing case for on paper...the strongest argument for in person...and the job where, when you hit the ground running, you won't trip over your shoelaces. Once you've decided on that job, build your universal resume with this in mind.

Now let me be clear – in most cases, universal resumes UNDER-PERFORM customized resumes by a wide margin. But they are extremely useful in these situations:

- **Job fairs:** Customized resumes are impractical for wide distribution at dozens of employer booths. That's why you should write the best universal, all-purpose resume you can and use it at job fairs. Then when you get a nibble from a company you'd like to work for, quickly get back to them with a more targeted resume. Going the extra mile like this makes you stand out from the competition.

- **Networking contacts:** Hand out universal resumes to your inner circle of friends to enable them to help you in your search. However, mark them: *"Confidential — For Your Eyes Only"* and ask them to contact you when they hear of job leads so you can respond with a job-specific, tailored resume.

- **LinkedIn:** When posted on social media sites like LinkedIn, it's best to use a universal approach with your resume and profile. Customization is tough because you don't know who'll be accessing your information and what they're looking for. So put your best foot forward.

- **Your References:** Send a generic or universal resume to people who have agreed to serve as a reference in your job search. It will serve to refresh them on your background.

- **For similar industries or sectors:** When you have a singular job goal — such as an HR position in only the banking or financial services industry — you can work with one really good resume directed at those sectors. But be prepared to adapt it later to a specific role.

Using Keywords in Your Universal Resume

Keywords are an important part of getting your resume noticed, as we mentioned in Chapter 1. Not only should you use keywords in your customized resume (as we'll discuss shortly), you should use it in your universal resume as well.

To illustrate, let's take LinkedIn. You should definitely place your universal resume on this site. And since most recruiters searching for candidates on LinkedIn do so through a keyword search, you should pay special attention to words and titles when posting your resume and filling out your profile there.

Let's say you're a Compensation & Employee Benefits Manager and your resume or profile uses that exact terminology. You might also want to sprinkle terms like *"executive compensation"* or *"benefits administration"* throughout your resume or profile too so that they appear in keyword searches as well as *"compensation and benefits."* In other words, give real thought to alternative synonymous titles and terms, and utilize them.

The more effectively you can do this, the more likely your credentials will pop up in someone's search results.

Here's how to find the right keywords for your Universal resume:

Step 1: Use this list of HR keywords as a starting point. The list of possible HR keywords is practically endless and some keywords are seen more often in large organizations than small businesses. For example, small businesses might use *"recruitment and selection,"* while large organizations employ phrases such as *"talent acquisition."* In any event, based on studies by LinkedIn, Career Builder and various HR executive search services, the top 50+ keywords in Human Resources are:

- ❑ Annual Appraisals
- ❑ Assessment & Selection
- ❑ Behavioral Interviewing
- ❑ Benchmarking
- ❑ Benefits Administration
- ❑ Career Development

- Change Management
- Coaching / Mentoring
- Collective Bargaining
- Compensation
- Contract Negotiations
- Culture Change
- Curriculum Development
- Diversity / Inclusion
- Employee Engagement
- Employee Handbook
- Employee Relations
- Employee Retention
- Employee Surveys
- Executive Search
- Facilitation
- Grievances
- Health & Safety Programs
- Health Care Programs
- HR Policies & Procedures
- HRIS / HR Information Systems
- Human Capital Management
- Job Descriptions
- Labor Relations
- Leadership Development
- Mentoring
- Mergers & Acquisitions
- Organizational Development
- Orientation
- Pay For Performance
- Pension Administration
- Performance Management
- Personnel Records
- Professional Development
- Program Design
- Recruitment / Staffing
- Regulatory Compliance
- Rewards & Recognition

- ❏ Salary Reviews
- ❏ Strategic HR Planning
- ❏ Succession Planning
- ❏ Talent Acquisition
- ❏ Talent Management
- ❏ Training & Development
- ❏ Vendor Management
- ❏ Workforce Planning

While the above may be helpful, it doesn't cover every HR-related keyword on earth and there's certainly no ONE single list of keywords that works for every single HR job. So, for that reason, it's helpful to go to…

Step 2: Use LinkedIn to review the profiles of your HR peers in other organizations and note the keywords that are used repeatedly. You can also review 5-10 employment ads with similar job titles to yours in HR and see which words are mentioned consistently. Once you see a keyword pattern, highlight them and be sure to include them in your resume and cover letter. Besides the specific areas of HR expertise noted in Step 1, keywords also tend to fall into these additional categories:

- Years of experience
- Required degrees or certifications
- Previous HR job titles
- Previous accomplishments or results attained
- Preferred HR skills and competencies
- Company or industry names
- University or college majors

Step 3: Based on the previous steps, pinpoint 6-12 keywords and make sure you include these in your resume. After making your keyword list and checking it twice, chances are you'll have more than 8 keywords to utilize. Perfect! Just be sure not to make every other word in your resume a keyword – too much of a good thing is painful, and no one wants to read a resume riddled with buzzword overkill – so start with your top 8 keywords and go from there.

When you've landed on your keywords, now integrate them into your universal resume format. When including them as statement of your experience, it's a good idea to start with an action verb and end with numbers, facts and figures.

Now with your universal resume in hand, you're ready for…

Resume #2
YOUR CUSTOMIZED RESUME

This type of resume takes your Universal one and adapts it to more precisely fit the requirements of each position you are ap-plying for. The goal in doing this is to convey that you're a perfect match for that job. The good news is that this will rarely require a major rewrite of your universal resume. Most times it will simply mean that you should:

#1: Change the job target or title in the Summary section. Always revise your target job title so that it reflects the EXACT position title for which you are applying. This way, there's no confusion about the position you want. You can see examples of how this is done by viewing the Martinez and Johnson resumes in Chapter 11.

#2: Customize the Summary statement and keywords. You want your Summary to be instantly perceived as a terrific match for the targeted job. This may mean moving your most relevant experience, skills and accomplishments to this section of your resume. You will want to ensure that the targeted job's most relevant 5-8 keywords are contained in this section too.

#3: Reword your accomplishment statements. Look at the-se bulleted statements of your Experience and ensure that the most essential words matching the job appear at the beginning of the bullet. This helps your resume pop in the minds of those who are scanning through the document quickly.

#4: Reorder the bullet points. Sequence your bullet points for each position so the most relevant and important for that po-sition are listed first. For example, if you have experience in recruiting software engineers and you're applying for a position which requires this as a must, those bullet points should go first. The same is true for the other experiences deemed as critical for the job. Bullet point as many of them as is applicable, in order of importance, from most relevant first to least relevant last. Again, this will ensure your most pertinent qualifications stand out.

#5: Mirror the language in the job posting. If you're applying for an HR job that has been posted, read it (or the job description) CAREFULLY and take the exact terminology or key words used in it and include them on your resume. For example, if a job posting says: *"Manage a staff of four human resources managers and professionals,"* make sure your resume reflects that you have managed a staff of HR professionals. Clearly spell out that you are the one for the position and don't leave them to ponder why they should consider you for the job. Most applicants never seem to fully read the job description.

Here five more suggestions to guide your customizing efforts:

#6: Use contacts or insiders. If you have a contact that works in the organization, that's golden. Use them to get additional information or the inside scoop on the job. Often posted jobs are quite generic and not written by the person actually feeling the pain (the hiring manager). So investigate the opportunity further with someone elsewhere in the HR organization other than the hiring authority. These folks can give you lots of information about what's needed. The more job specifics you can get, the better you can target your resume

#7: Get inside the employer's head. If there's not available information on the job, think like the employer. Examine what you believe might be of value to them. For example, if you've read about a company that is fending off an attempt to unionize by the Teamsters, you could emphasize that aspect of your employee relations experience citing how you've helped your previous firms successfully deal with union organizing attempts.

#8: Use mission linking. Tying the content of your resume to the company's mission statement is a unique technique for connecting with a prospective employer. Corporate PR departments can provide this information, as can the company's website. Use this info to show how your experience or professional aspirations can contribute to accomplishing the company's goals, purposes, or values. You can do this in your Summary statement at the top of the resume.

#9: Probe for more details. If someone talks to you about a specific job that you're interested in, avoid giving out your universal resume so quickly. Instead, probe and ask them lots of questions about the role and then offer to email a customized version of it to them later. You might find out, for example, that the role requires extensive experience in compensation redesign or health care cost containment which you can then emphasize on the resume you send.

#10: Include a customized cover letter. After you have tailored your resume to the job you want. If a cover letter is needed, be sure to customize it as well. You want to make it as easy as possible for the recruiter to know you have what they need. You might even provide a two-column summary with the organization's needs on the left and how you meet or exceed those needs on the right. (You will find more information about cover letters in Chapter 14.)

Example:
USING KEYWORDS TO CUSTOMIZE YOUR
RESUME FOR A SPECIFIC HR JOB

Previously we discussed how to keyword optimize your Universal resume. Let's now discuss how to customize the keywords in your resume for a specific position.

On the next page (Exhibit 3-1) you'll see an open position description for an HR Director. In this example, I've underlined the 8 keywords that match the applicant's skills best.

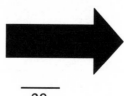

Exhibit 3-1: Underlined Keywords for an Open HR Position

DIRECTOR - HUMAN RESOURCES
Emerging Foods Division, XYZ Corp

Overview:
The Director of Human Resources (HR) is responsible for leading and managing all HR programs, labor relations and talent retention and development initiatives for the U.S. Emerging Foods Division of XYZ.

This role supports the sales headquarters and eight food manufacturing locations in the U.S., Canada & Mexico. The ideal candidate will be a strong leader, an impactful HR generalist partner, resourceful and have excellent interpersonal and communications skills. The position reports to the General Manager, U.S. Emerging Markets with a strong dotted line to the Vice-President of Human Resources, XYZ Corp.

Qualifications and Professional Attributes:
- Masters Degree preferred in Human Resources, Labor Relations or a related discipline.
- Minimum of 7+ years experience as a successful HR generalist partner or consultant role with multiple clients in multiple locations.
- Labor relations experience is crucial as the workforce is 80% unionized and is represented by five labor unions.
- Minimum of 2 years of project management experience including project plan development and tracking.
- Strong leadership, project management & prioritization skills are required.
- Prefer prior HR Management experience in the food manufacturing industry.
- Experience defining developing and implementing employee engagement programs that can improve sales and/or manufacturing productivity.
- Highly developed presentation and influence skills gained by working work with front-line employees, sales headquarters staff and senior level executives.

Now here's how to use those 8 underlined keywords (along with some "additional" keywords also contained in the job description) to create bullets for your customized resume:

Underlined Keywords: *labor relations*
Additional Keywords: *labor unions*
Customized Bullet For Your Resume:
- Served as the **labor relations** Chief Spokesperson and helped negotiate three **labor union contracts** on time, 5% on average below budgeted contract costs and without business interruptions or work stoppages.

Underlined Keywords: *talent retention, employee engagement*
Additional Keywords: *sales headquarters*
Customized Bullet For Your Resume:
- Helped improve **talent retention** of our key **sales headquarters** staff by 16% over the prior year through mentoring and other customized **employee engagement** initiatives.

Underlined Keywords: *Masters degree*
Additional Keywords: *Human Resources*
Customized Bullet For Your Resume:
- Graduated with a **Masters degree** in **Human Resources**, with high honors, from Purdue University.

Underlined Keywords: *Human Resources generalist partner, food manufacturing industry*
Additional Keywords: *years experience*
Customized Bullet For Your Resume:
- 10 **years experience** as a **Human Resources generalist partner** for 3 organizations --including the 2nd largest plant in the **food manufacturing industry.**

Underlined Keywords: *Leadership, project management*
Additional Keywords: none used
Customized Bullet For Your Resume:

- Provided HR **leadership** and **project management** support **for** a work simplification initiative that saved $3.2 million in reduced headcount and reduced non-valued added work over 11 months.

As you can see, investing the time to add relevant keywords to re-shape your resume positions you as a highly qualified candidate for this job. It can differentiate you from the others that didn't make the extra effort to do this.

Final Thoughts on Keyword Customizing Your Resume

- **For maximum impact, incorporate the keywords in the upper third of page one of your resume.** That will significantly elevate your chances of attracting the employers' interest in your candidacy. You'll want to especially ensure that you include them in your "Summary" at the top of your resume and in your cover letter so they'll be recognized.

- **When you use acronyms, spell them out.** Example: FMLA (Family & Medical Leave Act). That's especially helpful since the person tasked with going through resumes might not know all the relevant abbreviations.

- **Avoid fuzzy keywords and phrases.** These include *customer-oriented, excellent communication skills, integrity,* and *character.* Yes, I did use *leadership* in the previous example, but it was backed up with a compelling and quantifiable accomplishment. In most cases, using these types of fuzzy words and phrases lack meaning and will do absolutely nothing to help you progress to the interview stage.

Now that we've covered the importance of having two types of resumes and how to incorporate keywords to customize them, let's now move on to how to best deliver your credentials to maximize your chances of getting interviewed.

4

Strategy Three:
PLAN TO DELIVER YOUR HR RESUME
3 WAYS FOR MAXIMUM EXPOSURE
TO HIRING AUTHORITIES

To get your HR resume read, it must fit an employer's requirements, not yours! You can be a perfect candidate, but if your
resume is delivered in the *wrong* format, your efforts are wasted.

In today's competitive job market, there are three methods (or
ways) for delivering your HR resume to elevate your chances of
it being favorably considered by hiring authorities:

Method 1: Provide a printed, full-design resume.
Method 2: Submit an ATS-optimized resume.
Method 3: Post or upload your resume online.

This chapter will give you the details on what you should do to
successfully execute each of these methods.

Delivery Method #1:
PROVIDE A PRINTED, FULL-DESIGN RESUME.

Even the most tech-savvy companies still like to receive traditional paper or printed resumes and you should be prepared to

deliver yours in that format. Even with today's technology, there are many companies who don't search for candidates online, even on business-oriented sites such as LinkedIn.

As long as printers continue to be made and people enjoy holding reading material in their hands, the traditional printed version of your full-design resume with be with us and will predominate. Human eyes find printed, full-design resumes far more inviting to read than any other type of resume. And you need to have this "attractive" version of your resume available to hand out when required.

All of the example resumes in Chapter 11 are printed, full-design resumes and were prepared using MS Word.

Here are the key points to remember about this version of your resume.

Paper
It should be printed on standard 8 ½" x 11" (letter-size) paper. The paper you choose should be conservative and distinctive, especially for HR leadership and executive candidates. White, off-white or very pale gray are the best choices. They are straightforward, no-nonsense colors that speak directly to your professionalism, assuming you want to be perceived as straightforward and no-nonsense.

Don't go overboard and use papers with watermarks (pictures, marble shades, or speckles). If your resume is scanned it can interpret these patterns and dots as letters. This is a good rule to follow even for paper resumes that will never be scanned. Often, companies will photocopy your resume to hand to a hiring manager, and dark colors or patterns will simply turn into dark masses that make your resume difficult to read. If a company has multiple locations, the original resume may even get faxed from one site to another and the same thing will happen.

Once in a while, I've seen HR resumes written on colored paper, paper with cutesy backgrounds and others are printed in italics or with some flowers in the margins. Please don't do this! These are resume gimmicks that may amuse the recipient but will likely eliminate your resume automatically.

Format

Prepare and maintain it in a **Word .doc** (or .docx) format. Most third party recruiters and headhunters prefer receiving it this way because it's good looking -- and it allows them to add their logo or brand and contact information to it.

Also, have a **PDF version** to attach to e-mails when providing them to contacts, colleagues and others in your network.

Fonts

Avoid fancy layouts, complicated fonts, and other special effects. Below are fonts I'd recommended:

Arial	Garamond
Book Antiqua	Georgia
Century Gothic	Gill Sans MT
Century Schoolbook	Tahoma
CG Omega	Times New Roman

Most resumes I've seen use Times New Roman, but it's overused. Your goal should be to create a competitively advantaged document that stands out, so take time to explore some of the alternative fonts above (I personally prefer Georgia).

Type Size

Clarity and readability are everything! As a general rule, select a 10 to 12 point font size. It's fine to go larger for your name, the companies you've worked for, and perhaps your titles. But be consistent. Too much font size variation creates a cluttered look.

The content, format and length of your resume should determine which font and font size you use. Some fonts look better than others at smaller or larger sizes. Some examples:

Tough to read in 9-point Times Roman

Collaborated with department leaders to implement a 15% rightsizing within their groups, saving $2.6 million. Provided managerial coaching, employee transition counseling and survivor assistance which minimized disruption to the business.

More comfortable to read in 11-point Georgia

Collaborated with department leaders to implement a 15% rightsizing within their groups, saving $2.6 million. Provided managerial coaching, employee transition counseling and survivor assistance which minimized disruption to the business.

Too large in 12-point Bookman Old Style

Collaborated with department leaders to implement a 15% rightsizing within their groups, saving $2.6 million. Provided managerial coaching, employee transition counseling and survivor assistance which minimized disruption to the business.

As you create your resume, play around with a few different fonts and sizes to see which ones best enhance your document.

Type Highlighting
It's ideal to use **bold**, CAPITALIZATION, *italics* and <u>underlining</u> and to highlight certain words, phrases, contributions, projects and other information you want to draw attention to. However, don't over use them.

Graphics
Keep graphics conservative or don't use them at all. Complicated tables, text boxes, and graphs might impress you, but often they get scrambled or eliminated when e-mailing your resume.

Number of Pages
The rules for printed, full-design HR resumes are simple:
- **Use one page** if you're a new graduate.
- **Use two pages max** for management-level candidates and those with 5 years of experience or more. This includes "C-level" executives (such as chief HR officer, chief talent officer and other HR chiefs).

This 1-2 page rule is an accepted business practice and has existed for years. Frankly, most U.S.-based executives outside of academia have neither the time nor attention span to read anything longer than two pages. And, any resume with more than this in the corporate world just raises red flags because it violates one of its basic purposes: to be <u>succinct.</u>

However, there are some caveats to the 1-2 page number rule:

- **Don't use tiny font sizes.** The worst crime you can commit is to use small fonts (9 points or less) just to squeeze your work history down into one or two pages. Do this and you'll piss off everyone who wears contacts or glasses for reading -- like me. Busy senior managers will simply refuse to read your resume because it speaks to poor judgment and communication skills, both of which are mandatory for prime time HR professionals.

- **Don't sacrifice relevance to the target job just to hit the right page number.** With electronic resumes in particular, the more job-specific keywords you're able to use, the better your chances of being selected in a keyword search. So, if you're a new college grad it is better to have a two-page resume with all the right keywords, skills and qualifications included than it is to have a one-page resume with information missing because you tried to fit page guidelines.

- **Back-up documents.** It's just fine to prepare a third page (or more) that's a separate document that you will present <u>ONLY</u> if it's requested -- like a list of your references or a longer version of your resume (2-3 pages) if more detail is asked for in your follow-up interviews.

- **Outside of the U.S., it's a different story.** In many foreign countries the resume is more like the U.S. academic CV. Page limit guidelines vary. Some even require information illegal to request in the U.S. Because of this, international rules are beyond the scope of this book.

Candidly, I often get push back on the 1-2 page rule. Opponents argue that HR jobs are getting increasingly more technical, complex and regulatory requiring much more detail. Also, the need for data-dense resumes (which are overwhelmingly rewarded in database searches), will make it a continuing challenge to limit the length of your resume on the basis of traditional guidelines developed before the age of computers.

All of those arguments are certainly entirely true. But ignore them! Here's why: your resume is not a book. It's simply an ad. And the most successful ads capture the reader's attention quickly, concisely and describe why someone should want to buy the product (you).

You want your 1-2 page resume to entice the hiring authority into asking for additional information -- that will, of course, necessitate him or her having to reach out to you to talk further or to set up an interview. *That's success! And it's also the number one goal of your resume.* Once they contact you, your resume has done its job. You can then provide them as much additional information as they'd like.

White Space
Finally, don't forget to allow for a reasonable amount of white space. Some resumes are so "cluttered" they never get read. Your resume needs to be pleasing to the eye, whether printed out or on a computer screen. So add as much white space as possible to enhance readability.

Delivery Method #2:
SUBMIT AN ATS-OPTIMIZED RESUME

The paper version of your resume is <u>not</u> sufficient. You should also prepare a version of your resume optimized for submission to applicant tracking systems (ATS). As I mentioned previously, ATSs are data management systems used by organizations to manage the flood of applications they receive. The ATS will read your resume and then rank and score your qualifications against the job description key words. Only those applicants whose resumes receive high scores will get called for interviews.

Exhibit 4-1: An Example ATS-Optimized Resume

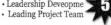

CANDACE COOPER
1234 N. Main Street
Atlanta, GA 12345
(555) 555-5558
candace.cooper@email.cc

PROFILE SUMMARY

HUMAN RESOURCES MANAGEF ... ts out and champions breakthrough ideas and initiatives. Quickly analyzes complex workplace probl ... inds actionable, pragmatic solutions. Able to take tough stands and resolve difficult business and people issues effectively. Skilled in:

- Talent Management   •Employee Relations   • Leadership Deveopme
- Work/Life Initiatives   •Organization Development   • Leading Project Team

EXPERIENCE

Imagemax, Inc – MANAGER –HUMAN RESOURCES [6/2013] – Present
Global leader in creating still imagery and online media products.

Provided human resources leadership and guidance for 400 managers and graphic designers in the Online Media Group. Reporting jointly to HR Senior Director and GM of Online Media.

- Proactively created "Leadership Roundtables" and identified 14 online programs to accelerate the orientation and development of new managers. Results: 95% utilization rate and positive feedback.

- Selected by Corporate Global HR to lead a 5-person project team to update the corporate policy on flexible work arrangements. Outcomes: Full policy e ... mproved retention annually by 3 percentage points or $3.3 million.

- Collaborated with department leaders to imp ... 15% rightsizing within their groups, saving $2.6 million. Provided managerial coaching, employee transition counseling and survivor assistance which minimized disruption to the business.

- Contributed to a 12% reduction in the number of monthly employee complaints filed and a reduction of management time spent on such complaints by driving 6 improvements in Online Media's utilization of the company-wide job posting process.

- On last two 360 results, scored 94%+ positive on the "quality, effectiveness and timeliness of HR support provided to clients" (detailed documentation provided upon request).

Previous Related Experience:

SUPERVISOR - WORKPLACE EFFECTIVENESS, APPLE [5/2011] – [6/2013]
SENIOR HUMAN RESOURCES ANALYST, AMAZON [4/2009] – [5/2011]
HUMAN RESOURCES ANALYST, AMAZON [6/2007] – [4/2009]

EDUCATION

M.S. Organization Psychology, Purdue University
B.S. Human Resources, Cornell University

CERTIFICATIONS

Certification, Leadership Architect Facilitator, Lominger Internal, Minneapolis, MN
Certification, Targeted Selection System, Development Dimensions

ATSs are used by most large employer websites like PepsiCo, Google, Procter & Gamble as well as at online resume sites and job boards like Career Builder and Monster. Studies continue to indicate that the majority of qualified job seekers are eliminated because their resumes don't comply with ATS rules – all of which start with submitting an ATS-optimized resume. This reliance on ATS systems is, at the moment, much stronger than any reliance on Facebook, Twitter, LinkedIn and other social media sites. If you were a recruiter, would you rather hunt through thousands of tweets for the one person you need for that Organization Development position or use an ATS to evaluate the resumes sent to you?

You can see an example of an ATS-optimized resume in the prior page (Exhibit 4-1). With that as your guide, here are the simple steps for creating one:

Use a standard Word document. Don't use templates. Be sure to save it in a **.doc** format (Word 97-2003). Not all ATSs can read .docx, PDF, RTF and JPG documents. Also use simple formatting: no headers, footers, templates, borders, lines, symbols or shading. Bullet points are fine.

Put your name on the top line followed by your contact information. Don't list your certifications or credentials (SPHR, MSHR, MBA, etc.) next to your name. Include that information in your Profile Summary or in the Education section of your resume.

Use a PROFILE SUMMARY (or EXECUTIVE SUMMARY) header after your contact information. Below this, put your other section headers (EXPERIENCE, EDUCATION, etc.) in ALL CAPS to make it easy for the ATS to categorize the information.

When applying for a specific position, DO use that exact job title on the resume. Be specific on the precise position you're seeking – for instance, note the use of "HUMAN RESOURCES MANAGER" in this example.

Use position keywords in your Profile Summary – and bullet them out so that they're even more clear.
If the job has been posted or currently available, incorporate the language, keywords and important phrases from the job description.

Format your work history correctly. Start with the employer's name, followed by your title and then the dates you held the title. The company name should be followed by Inc., Corp., LLC or something similar so the system can identify it as a company. You should also have these three components next to each other to ensure it's understood by the ATS. If you wish to include a context statement describing the organization you worked with, DO include that statement after the organization name, your title, and employment dates (see the example).

Note too that if you have held multiple positions at the same company, you need to repeat the company name again.

Use keywords and phrases *in context*. Incorporate and spread them into your accomplishment bullet points throughout your resume. Do not just include them in your Profile Summary. (See Chapter 3 for additional information on how to customize keywords).

Here are some additional guidelines for ATS optimization:

1. Use basic looking fonts (Arial, Georgia, Tahoma, Calibri, and Verdana are best choices).
2. Make sure the font sizes are visible (11 point font or above).
3. Don't mix different fonts and sizes in your resume.
4. Include no punctuation in your name, such as ( ) , / -.

5. Use the full, spelled-out version of terms in addition to abbreviations and acronyms [e.g. Fair Labor Standards Act (FLSA)]
6. DON'T feel the need to create a completely stripped down document. In the old days, candidates would save documents in .txt format with absolutely no formatting before submitting online. However, because your resume will eventually be seen by a human being, keep some simple formatting such as bold, caps and bullet points to add to the attractiveness of your resume.
7. Edit carefully. The ATS will not recognize misspelled words. And, if your resume survives the ATS screen, it will next be reviewed by human beings so it must be ~~Eror~~ error-free
8. DO check your email after applying for a position online. Some applicant tracking systems acknowledge submissions, but these automated responses may be diverted to your spam folder (so check that too).
9. If given the choice, DO upload your resume rather than cutting pasting sections into text boxes. When it is eventually forwarded to a human, it will look much more attractive.
10. DO feel free to make your resume as long as you want to. ATSs don't penalize you for length. However, since it may also be read by a person, trying very hard to keep it to two pages max is smart. However, if you have a 2-page resume, put your name and Page 2 in a header (that way, the ATS can't misinterpret it).

In summary, understand that there are hundreds of different systems out there, and they all operate slightly differently. Your goal is to do your best to simplify the formatting while still providing keyword-rich, achievement-oriented bullet points.

That's the story on how to best deliver an ATS-optimized resume. Let's now more on to...

Delivery Method #3
POST OR UPLOAD YOUR RESUME ONLINE

There are four key places for delivering your resume online.

Place Number One: LINKEDIN
Hands down, this is number one. It's used by 300+ million people globally and by employers around the world who search for HR talent. Don't fool with **Facebook, Twitter** or any other social media sites…they will waste your time. Focus instead on the recruiter's favorite: LinkedIn.

LinkedIn gives you a "profile" page on which you can write anything about yourself and your work history using the standardized template that they provide. *This profile page acts as your "resume" on LinkedIn.* To fill out your profile page, transfer (or cut and paste) information directly to it from your UNIVERSAL RESUME.

In addition, follow these nine powerful LinkedIn tips if you want your profile page to attract <u>more</u> potential opportunities:

#1: Include a professional-looking PHOTO. This is an absolute must. Every job search study has shown that not having a professional-looking photo as part of your profile turns off most employers. According to LinkedIn, with a photo you are *7 times MORE likely* to be found in employer searches. So make sure you have one and that it provides a flattering shot of your head and shoulders. The picture should be sharp, clear and well lit, even if taken with a smart phone. Be sure to dress up. And smile.

#2: Make sure your profile is 100% COMPLETE. If your profile is not 100% complete, you'll know because LinkedIn will bug you to death every time you log in until it's done. Don't question them – just do it!

Here's why: the payoff is huge. According to LinkedIn, because of the way their search function works, your profile will be *40 times more likely to be viewed by employer searches if it's 100% complete.* Wow! That's 40 times the opportunities. So if you want to get better results, completing your profile is one of the easiest paths to success. If your profile is not fully complete, go to the LinkedIn Profile Completeness page and follow the simple instructions there. It will only take a few minutes.

#3: In your HEADLINE, provide a searchable JOB TITLE and compelling ELEVATOR PITCH. To clarify, your headline is located immediately under your name on your profile. And it's the first thing a headhunter, recruiter or hiring manager sees, after your name and picture.

Here's the deal: most employers search LinkedIn by job title and industry. So, to dramatically increase your chances that an employer's search will pick you up, list your current job title in the headline section…follow it with a slash…and then add the industry you want to find a job in.

Examples:

> Director, Human Resources | Financial Services
> Compensation Manager | Food & Beverages
> Vice President, Talent Management | Healthcare

If your current job title does not contain words that would normally be used to search for someone who does what you do, first put in a slash mark…then add an *equivalent title* they would use…and lastly add the industry.

Example:

> HR Business Partner | Manager, Human Resources | Retail

Now, to make your headline compelling, turn it into a short *elevator pitch* that really grabs a recruiter's attention by adding:
1. Your ROLE.
2. WHO you help.
3. HOW you make organizations better.
4. PROOF that you are credible.

Examples:

Senior Manager, Talent Acquisition | Technology
Helps high-tech firms recruit top IT talent faster.
Results featured in HR Magazine.

Director, Human Resources | Consumer Products
Helps manufacturing firms boost workforce engagement.
P&G President's Award Winner.

Organization Development Consultant | Oil & Energy
Helps R&D executives grow their future leaders.
Clients include Exxon & Chevron.

Notice how with the addition of a few short statements (i.e. an elevator pitch), you can differentiate yourself from the rest of the ho-hum HR crowd and make your profile pop. Again, these are just examples. You can certainly craft one that's much better than these. However, you'll need to be brief because LinkedIn only provides 120 characters for your headline. So take full advantage of this valuable space to create an enticing headline..

#4: Make the SUMMARY section sizzle. This section can contain up to 2000 characters. Use this space to expand on the elevator pitch in your Headline and make sure it's consistent with the Summary in your Universal Resume (see Chapter 6). It should overview your experience, credentials, expertise, personal values, work ethic, background or anything that qualifies you for the ideal job you're going after. Most importantly, it should hook the reader into *continuing to read your profile.*

Important: Below the Summary section is a subheading called **SPECIALTIES.** Think of this area as your pantry full of keywords that you want to be searched by. In it, include the 8-12 keywords you developed for your Universal Resume (see Chapter 3) and any others that are relevant. This is another way to ensure your name will come up highly in search results and help recruiters with applicable HR opportunities find you.

#5: Add 5 to 8 RECOMMENDATIONS. Contact former bosses, clients, managers and classmates and ask them to access your profile and provide recommendations. These types of endorsements give you an edge in situations where you lack certain qualifications or have less experience than other candidates.

#6: Provide your PHONE NUMBER and your E-MAIL ADDRESS. Yes, I know this seems minor. But most people don't include this information because they don't want to be bothered. Get over it! Include all your contact data to make it easy for potential interviewers to connect with you.

#7: Add links to any WEBSITES that help you stand out. This includes: (a) Your blog, if you have one, and ONLY if the posts there are relevant to your area of HR expertise; and (b) The personal web page where you keep your full-design universal resume. If you don't have a website, use the LinkedIn feature that allows you to upload your resume in MS Word or PDF.

#8: Join one or more LINKEDIN GROUPS, related to the area of your HR expertise and start COMMENTING. Do this sparingly but often, when they are discussing something you are an expert on. This builds your HR reputation. People who post get *four times the profile views* of those who don't.

#9: Copy and paste your WORK EXPERIENCE and EDUCATION sections directly from your Universal Resume. This is critical. It ensures your resume and Profile line up.

LinkedIn deservedly merits significant attention. Let's now cover three more places you should deliver your resume online:

Place Number Two: YOUR OWN PERSONAL WEBSITE
Upload your full-design resume to your own personal website. Your own site lets you text or email the link where your resume is located to recruiters, where it can be accessed from their **tablets, smart phones** or other **mobile devices.** This enables you to

respond fast to HR opportunities. No fumbling with electronic documents, which can waste time. To get your own free website, google "free personal websites" or "free resume websites."

Place Number Three: HR POSITIONS POSTED ONLINE
If you're applying for positions posted online at company websites or job boards, check out their submission requirements first. If there is an "Import Resume" or "Browse" button, you can upload your full-design resume in either MS doc form or PDF form. If not, use an ATS-optimized resume and embed a link to your LinkedIn profile; or the URL of your personal website so they have a link to your full-design resume as well. In any event, be sure to follow their instructions to the letter.

Place Number Four: RECRUITING FIRM WEBSITES
When delivering your resume electronically to headhunters, use your full-design resume. Most prefer receiving good looking resumes in a word doc format so they can alter them if needed. However, always verify the preferred format with them first.

Caution: If an agency recruiter sees that you have your own personal website, they may be reluctant to work with you. Some employers have claimed that putting your resume on your own website puts it in public domain and have used that as rationale to avoid paying the placement agency. So, be totally open with the firm about where you've posted your resume.

To conclude, use all three of these forms of your resume (printed, ATS-optimized, online) to get it disseminated. A paper version of your resume alone will not suffice. New technology is allowing access to resume information through websites, ATSs, smart phones, tablets and other devices.

This means you need to deliver your resume so that it is readable by hiring authorities (and anyone else) using these technologies. Don't get left behind. Get your resume into as many places as possible, both online and offline, and it will exponentially increase your chances of landing interviews.

SIX RULES FOR WRITING A DYNAMITE HR RESUME THAT OPENS DOORS & WOWS 'EM EVERY TIME!

Rule #1:
Lead With The Right Contact Information

Rule #2:
Hook The Reader With Your Summary

Rule #3:
Sell Your HR Experience Powerfully

Rule #4:
Add Punch & Pop To Your Formal Education

Rule #5:
Use Resume Boosters To Set Yourself Apart
From Your Competition

Rule #6:
Make Sure It Can Pass The 15-Second
Scan Test

5

Rule One:
LEAD WITH THE RIGHT
CONTACT INFORMATION

It's now time to start writing your resume. Frankly, this isn't high on the fun list for most HR pros. However, once your resume is done, it will remind you of all that you've accomplished and I guarantee you'll view it with self-satisfaction and pride.

To make the writing process easier and more efficient, I've laid out six simple rules that you should follow. And that starts with your **contact information.** This is an important part of your resume because it clarifies how you can be reached.

Below is **one** of the *many* different ways it can be displayed at the top of your resume:

JIM CARRINGTON
444 Rhodes Drive • Asheville, NC 29615
(444) 449.7474 • jcarrington11@gmail.com

Now let's breakdown the key components:

<u>Your Name</u>
Place your name first on the very top line of your resume. In the above example, if your actual name isn't on that first line, a

computer may mistake Rhodes Drive as your name and file you away as Mr. Drive. Also, use the name you want to be known by...for example: "Jim Carrington" and not "James Edward Harold Carrington, III." You want it to stand out and be easy to read -- so putting it in bold and in a size range of 14- to 16-point typeface should do the trick.

As an additional differentiator, you may also want to consider showcasing your HR-related certifications behind your name at the top of your resume as follows:

Barbara Smyth, SPHR, CCP
Jonathan Carrington, PHR

Here's why. About 11% of HR professionals globally have HR-related certifications, based on recent numbers published by SHRM. That's a big enough percentage and an elite enough group to make some HR hiring authorities take such certifications seriously. So, if you're part of this group, showcase it!

However, many HR folks don't believe they should highlight their certifications in such a blatant way on their resumes. If you're in that group I understand. However, here's why I think you should:

- First of all, if you don't, no one else will. My philosophy is that there are two places in your career where it doesn't pay to be modest: during your performance review and when seeking a new job.
- Secondly, you've worked hard to get HR certified and it represents a career-long commitment that shows hiring authorities and future employers that you have mastered the core HR principles and that you are dedicated to staying current in our profession. To me, it's similar to a CPA for Accounting & Finance professionals. And that's exactly how you should sell it in your interviews.

You will want to emphasize your certifications in the Education section of your resume also (see the examples in Chapter 7).

On the other hand, let me not blow smoke. The jury is still out on the value of a PHR, SPHR, CCP or any HR-related certifications. There's no evidence that they will help you land your dream job. But they won't kill your chances either...and may give you that itty-bitty edge that allows your résumé to hit the "yes" stack. And that's all you can reasonably expect.

(Full disclosure: I'm not HR-certified myself. But I recognize the value it has in the eyes of some in validating your HR expertise and differentiating you from those who don't have it. Besides, putting those initials behind your name is kinda cool.)

Your Physical Home Address
More and more candidates are ditching the physical address *entirely*...and using only their name, e-mail address and phone number as contact information at the top of their resume. The rationale: it's not often you'll be using snail mail to get your resume to someone and similarly employers will likely not be communicating with you by traditional mail either.

However, I do recommend including it just as you see in the Jim Carrington example on the page 59. Why? Because it's still important to convey to many employers the stability of physical home address. It's still important to ensure all the ways of reaching you are covered off. And finally, it's important that you not raise any unnecessary questions as to why you've excluded it.

Phone number
Use your mobile number. Most employers prefer to pick up phone and give you a call or text you. I do not recommend using your work number unless you have no other choice. You can't assume a caller will be discreet just because he/she is calling you on the job.

Caution: Whichever phone number you list, be sure to have a brief, professional-sounding voicemail greeting and check your messages often. Your voice message should say something like: *"This is Jane Doe at 555-555-5555. Please leave me a message and I'll get back to you as soon as I can. Thank you."* That's it. No music, no children's voices and no gimmicks. Avoid adding any inspirational message like: *"Have a blessed day"* or *"God bless you."* The intent is good, but it's risky during a job search. I suggest you go with the vanilla greeting and then, once you're hired, you can do anything you want with your voice mail.

Email address

This is an absolute must. Email is the primary form of communication between job seekers and recruiters/employers. Use a personal email address for your job search, not your work email. Not only could using your work email get you into trouble with your organization, it will also make a poor impression with a potential employer.

Caution: Avoid using a cutesy or hair-raising e-mail address on your resume. Sure, some recruiters will get a chuckle from out of viewing EvilHRLady@aol.com or JimBongBoy@cox.net -- but do you think employers really want to hire HR leaders that refer to themselves in this way? Obviously, these are extreme examples. But don't give a potential employer an easy reason to drop you from the process. You can quickly grab an email address from yahoo, gmail, hotmail or lots of other free providers...so there's no reason to use one that will raise red flags.

Mini-Contact Information on Page Two

If your resume is two pages, be sure to briefly carry your contact information to the second page. Just copy and paste the heading from page one onto the top of page two. Then delete all but your name, phone number and email address -- then add page 2. By doing this, if page one of your resume gets detached, it makes it easy for the recruiter to call or drop you a quick note requesting you email them this page. [Note: This also applies if you've elected to create a resume with three or more pages (which I wouldn't advise). Put mini headings at the top of all pages beyond page one.]

Having covered how to best lay out your contact information, let's now move to the more meaty sections of your resume.

6

Rule Two:
HOOK THE READER WITH
YOUR SUMMARY

Your resume needs a hook to grab attention. The best hook you can create is one that immediately follows your name and contact information and is expressed as either an *"Objective"* or as a *"Summary."*

I suggest only using a *"Summary."*

An *"Objective," "Career Objective,"* or anything along those lines is a complete waste of space. To illustrate why, here's one that I looked at recently....

NOT!

> **Objective**
> Seeking a challenging HR management opportunity
> with dynamic company that will lead to
> advancement opportunities.

This is trite, canned, and self-serving. It's also not specific. Who isn't looking for "challenging" work or "advancement opportunities"? What does "HR management" mean? What is a "dynamic company"? Bottom line, this statement uses a lot of words that raise questions and say nothing.

Here's another example:

> **NOT!**
>
> **Career Objective**
>
> Seeking an HR executive position with an emerging company that markets innovative products or services looking to rapidly expand.

Most organizations in the U.S. don't consider themselves "emerging companies." And many might well be afraid of a candidate who wants to join only a company "looking to rapidly expand." Again, another example of wasted words.

I'm sure these Career Objectives were important to the people who wrote them. But statements like these are fluff to hiring managers and will screen you out instantly. It's last decade's style. So beat them to the punch – take them out yourself.

Today's overworked hiring managers don't give a crap about *your* objectives. They only care about *their own* objectives. They're concerned about what you want only if it also gives them what *they* want. So, your #1 priority should be showing them how you will fill their needs, wants and desires -- not yours.

Examples of Winning Summary Statements

When I say "Summary," I mean a summary *for the job you're applying for.* It should contains three to four brief statements -- no more than 3-5 lines total -- that describes why you are the best candidate for the job in a way that is compelling enough to make the reviewer want to read more. That's all.

In your Summary section, you can write about your experience, credentials, expertise, personal values, work ethic, background, or anything that qualifies you for the job you're going for. You're free to make claims, drop names, and do your best to entice the reader to *keep reading your resume.* Remember, all your claims must be substantiated later when you write the body of the resume, so be honest while giving yourself full credit.

Below are some example Summary statements covering a variety of HR professionals:

For an HR generalist wanting to remain in California...

Summary
Certified Professional in Human Resources (PHR) and state certified in California (PHR-CA). 5+ years experience in attracting, developing and retaining engineering and IT talent in the Bay Area and Northern California.

For a fresh MBA grad seeking her first full-time HR job...

Profile Summary
Recent MBA graduate with concentration in Human Resources (4.0 GPA). Two summers of human resources intern experience with two Fortune 500 organizations, meeting aggressive deadlines on HR projects.

For an Employee Benefits Director...

Career Summary
Employee Benefits Leader with six years experience in a major hospital system, ranked 4th in the country by *U.S. News & World Report*. Led the team that restructured health care, retirement and wellness programs which delivered $7.5 million in annual savings.

For a Vice President - Global Talent Management...

Executive Summary
Global Senior Talent Management Executive skilled at collaborating with executive business leaders. Reputation for developing low-cost, high-impact global HR strategies that have contributed to 15%+ growth in both the U.S. and Asian markets.

For a Director - Training & Organization Development...

Summary
15+ years of **Organization Development** experience leading teams of 10-30 staff members. Managed 30+ client projects budgeted from $100K to $1.7M. 500+ hours teaching and training on a wide variety of subjects including leadership, teamwork and project management.

Think of your Summary statement as a classified ad that's designed to sell the hiring authority on why you should be interviewed. It's the backbone of your resume. You should use a Summary in these situations:

- **If you have at least five years of experience.** Clearly, this five-year benchmark is not a hard-and-fast rule (note the MBA graduate exception above)...it's just that after about five years in HR, you will have accumulated enough experience and accomplishments to warrant this type of synopsis of your career.

- **If you're pursuing an HR executive role.** The sheer breadth of your experience demands a summary, just as 200-page thesis calls for an introductory abstract.

- **If you've had a variety of very diverse HR roles.** A Summary of your qualifications will pull various similar or unique experiences and skills into one easy-to-digest paragraph.

- **If your most impressive accomplishments won't be seen until the latter part of the resume.** In this case, a Summary will position the meatiest part of your experience at the beginning of your resume.

- **If you are targeting a position that calls on experience found only in the early stages of your career.** Mentioning earlier experiences in a Summary will breathe new life into dated employment.

- **If your resume will have to pass the rigors of computer scanning software or internet search engines.** Although keywords can be found anywhere in a resume, it doesn't hurt to load them up in your Summary near the top of the page.

HOW TO CREATE DYNAMITE SUMMARY SENTENCES

Here are some questions and examples to help you come up with strong sentences to include as part of your Summary:

1. How much experience do you have in Human Resources or in your specialty?

Example: Someone pursuing comp & benefits opportunities might answer, "I've worked as a compensation and benefits manager for a mid-sized company for the last 10 years."

And, therefore could use this sentence in their Summary...

> Compensation and Benefits Manager with 10 years experience in an organization with revenues of $200 million

2. Imagine a close HR colleague of yours is talking to the hiring manager for the job you want. What would they say about you that would intrigue the employer?

Example: The colleague an HR job hunter desiring a leadership role with a bank might answer, "She even won the SHRM's HR Award for Excellence for her work on retaining talent in the banking services sector."

You could translate that into a Summary sentence which reads:

> Winner of the Society of Human Resource Management (SHRM) National Award for Excellence for retaining talent in banking services.

3. How is success measured for the position you want? How do you measure up?

Example: An HRIS specialist looking to stay in the same field might answer, "Many of my clients have told me that I'm able to break down and explain human resources systems and technology issues very simply so that they're easy to understand."

That could result in the following Summary sentence...

> Reputation for providing clear, concise and user-friendly explanations of HRIS and complex technology issues to clients.

4. What is it about your personality that makes this job a good fit for you?

Example: A labor relations manager seeking a Director-level role might answer, "In tough labor negotiations, I am very diplomatic, so I get good results."

And this could be a Summary sentence for him...

> As Chief Spokesman during labor negotiations, demonstrated top-notch diplomacy that consistently produced win-win results for the organization and its employees.

5. What personal commitments or passions do you have that would be valued by the employer?

Example: Someone seeking a key role in the talent development function in an organization might answer, "Committed to growing and helping leaders at all levels."

Here's a sample Summary sentence that could reflect this...

> Strong commitment to growing and developing leaders at all levels so that they reach their full-potential.

6. Do you have any technical, linguistic, or artistic talents that would be useful on the job?

Example: Someone applying for an international HR role might answer, "I can speak Spanish and Russian."

If so, they could include this sentence in their Summary...

> Multilingual -- Fluent in Spanish and Russian.

The bottom line: Good Summary statements chunk down your story and describe why you are best candidate in just a few short sentences. It's important that it be brief, compelling and employ sentences that compel hiring authorities to read further to get more details about you as a candidate. (For more Summary statements that can guide you in creating yours, see the resume examples provided in Chapter 11).

Tailoring Your Summary To An Available Position

In starting your resume with a Summary, you can still target it to a specific position by naming the position itself on the resume. To illustrate this, note the following two examples taken from resumes in Chapter 11.

MORGAN S. JOHNSON, PHR
10099 Carter Circle • Cleveland, OH 34788
Home (333) 449-1212 • Cell (454) 467-9044
mjjohnson@sbcglobal.net

CANDIDATE FOR HR DIRECTOR – AT CHEVRON

SUMMARY OF QUALIFICATIONS: **Human Resources Executive** with 11 years of proven experience working with senior management on Talent Management strategies which drive business results in oil and energy companies. Certified HR professional with broad knowledge of approaches to optimize talent in a variety of workplaces including corporate, sales, union and non-union environments. Proven track record and superior abilities in the following areas:

- Talent Management
- Training & Development
- Employee Relations
- Employee Retention
- Compensation & Benefits
- Change Management

JILL J. MARTINEZ
21455 Nixon Drive Bay City, MI 10029
jill_martinez@email.com (216) 897-3452

CANDIDATE FOR HR ANALYST,
INTERNATIONAL DIVISION -- AT CITIBANK

Summary of Qualifications:
Experience in job placement, recruiting and training. Intercultural sensitivity, having lived abroad in Europe for two years. Ability to represent the organization with professionalism and confidence. Multilingual, fluent in Spanish & French -- written, verbal and in presentations.

Notice how both Johnson and Martinez have tailored their resume's Summary section to the specific position title and company they're applying for. You'll want to do this in cases where you're applying for a specific job has been posted or in situations where you know the *exact title* for a job that's currently open.

In this Chapter, we've covered how to use your Summary to hook the reader. Let's now move on to how to best capture and position your professional experience.

7

Rule Three:
SELL YOUR PROFESSIONAL
EXPERIENCE POWERFULLY

Your *Professional Experience* is the meat of your resume. It's what gives your resume substance, power, meaning and depth. In just about all cases, it will take up the most space and describe your biggest selling points. If your Summary hooks the reader, then your Professional Experience must now reel him/her in.

With that in mind, a quick quiz: Which of the following two examples does the best job of selling the job candidate?

Professional Experience – Example #1

GLOBAL TELECOMMUNICATIONS, Columbus, Ohio

Director of Human Resources, West Coast Services: Responsible for providing HR generalist support to the West Coast telecommunications operations group. This included all employee and labor activities, (Chief Spokesperson for contract negotiations), union avoidance campaigns, wage and benefits planning, plant closures, workforce planning, coordination of all staffing and talent acquisition activities and the college recruiting process.

Professional Experience – Example #2

GLOBAL TELECOMMUNICATIONS, Columbus, Ohio

Director of Human Resources, West Coast Services:
Recruited to lead HR for the 8,500 employee West Coast operations group located in CA, OR and WA. Managed a $24 million budget with full generalist responsibilities for labor relations, union avoidance, compensation, staffing and talent acquisition. Exceeded performance expectations all four years with company:

- **Year 1:** As Chief Spokesman, negotiated the company's first-ever early union contract settlement with the Teamsters which lowered operations costs by $2.7 million. Won "Chairman's Award for HR Excellence."
- **Year 2:** Introduced weekly scorecards which increased employee engagement in the operations group from 40 to 76%. Process recognized as a company best practice and used in 26 other locations.
- **Year 3:** Helped drive initiatives which lowered absenteeism from 16% to 8% - which ranks #2 in the company.
- **Year 4:** Effectively used online sourcing strategies to improve cost per hire by 38% saving $238,000 in talent acquisition costs.

I'm guessing (and hoping) you'd say Example #2. Just to clarify, these are before and after versions representing the *same person!* Example #1 was a first draft written by her. Example #2 was written as a result of asking a series of targeted, sequenced questions...and strengthened by using *statistics, metrics* and *numbers* from her accomplishments to quantify and further prove her value.

Creating statements similar to those in Example #2 on your resume will provide punch, impact and will give you the edge over other competitors for the same position. And it is precisely what you should strive to do when it comes to communicating your professional experience.

I know what's going through your mind right now. You may think that if you've had the same position for 10 years, it's going to be tough to summarize everything you've done into one short section.

On the opposite end of spectrum, if you've had your position for only 11 months, it may seem impossible to make such little experience sound substantial and noteworthy.

Let me assure you right now, that it's not only possible, but I'm 100% confident you can do it!

Your key lies in your ability to:

- **Be selective.** Your resume is not a biography -- there's no need to describe everything you've done. That's a trap. Your goal is to briefly capture your experience and highlight only those "critical few" accomplishments that present you in the best light.

- **Avoid going back more than 15 years in your dates of employment.** Beyond fifteen years, nobody really cares. The world has massively changed since then. If you're concerned about omitting this information, then consolidate dates, companies and jobs beyond this time window.

- **Quantify your work experience, contributions and accomplishments.** Optically, the human eye is pulled towards quantifiable symbols (e.g., $, #, or %) and you should leverage that fact on your resume. Using numbers, rather than just words alone is the winning ticket to clarifying and adding power to your experience -- no matter how much or how little of it you've had.

On this latter point, let me clarify. This doesn't mean that you should ignore valuable contributions you've made that cannot be quantified. It simply means that you should *try to quantify your achievements every single time you possibly can.*

With that thought in mind, let's now cover a variety of different ways you can do this by discussing....

7 WAYS TO ENERGIZE AND STRENGTHEN THE VALUE OF YOUR HR CONTRIBUTIONS

First of all, I prefer to use "contributions" or "impact statements" because they are employer-oriented terms, whereas "accomplishments" and its synonyms tend to sound more candidate-focused.

That said, here are 7 ways to enhance the value of your HR contributions and elevate them to an entirely different level:

Way #1:
SHOW HOW YOU MADE OR SAVED MONEY FOR THE ORGANIZATION

Examples:
- Cut the Brand Manager cost-to-hire rate by 40% through improvements in using social media to attract candidates.
- Contributed to a reduction of 14% in the number of complaints filed per employee resulting in a $30,000 savings.
- Implemented leadership training for front-line supervisors saving $125,000 in outside consulting fees.
- Led the effort which won 2 union organizing campaigns which avoided $1.5MM in increased employment costs.
- Co-led year-long project to identify non-compliance OSHA issues and initiated appropriate remedial action. Results: Passed OSHA inspection with zero findings, avoiding $500K in potential cost penalties.

Way #2:
SHOW HOW YOU ENHANCED PRODUCTIVITY OR MADE WORK EASIER

Examples:
- Selected as the HR leader for the national team that merged 4 fragmented service centers into one, single centralized unit...which improved order-processing time across the company by 40%.

- Led the initiative to consolidate the Talent Review and Performance Review processes resulting in less duplication of data and a reduction of 14 hours of review time per manager -- without any loss of essential information.
- Collaborated with the new EVP to initiate employee Town Hall meetings and brown-bag lunches to gather input from all levels of the R&D organization. Ideas generated from the researchers and staff employees collectively improved documented productivity by 16%.
- Designed and implemented a new sales internship program that reduced the time spent on administration and "paper-work" by direct sales staff by 11% during peak periods.

Way #3:
SHOW HOW YOU SAVED TIME

Examples:
- Co-introduced HRIS technology that took new hire data transfers from a 2-day process to "real time" mode. Idea was subsequently adopted by company's 4 satellite offices.
- Reduced hiring time on "hard to fill" software engineering positions from 90 to 30 days through innovative use of LinkedIn and Twitter.
- Trained customer service staff on timesaving concepts from the classic *One-Minute Manager* and other personal readings. Team now has time for special projects that had been "on hold" for more than 6 months.
- Led, as change agent with the CFO, an analysis of work processes in financial services resulting in new protocols that reduced weekly cost report generation time by 75%.

Way #4:
SHOW HOW YOU WERE PROACTIVE AND LED

No matter what your HR role is, the ability to lead, influence and sell your ideas is extremely valuable.

HR folks with proven skills in taking charge, being proactive and leading are always in demand. If you don't believe you've led and you're seeking a role that calls for leadership skills, ask yourself how many times you were a leader of a project, a task force, a team, a meeting or even a small event.

It doesn't matter if you were never formally appointed as the boss or given a leadership title. If you've had success leading others, you should reference leadership as one of your attributes.

Sprinkle leadership terms throughout your resume, including sections covering your experience, education, and extracurricular activities.

Examples:

- Proactively led the development of a new attendance policy which has reduced absenteeism levels at the Peterborough location by 2% year-on-year
- Led the HR team which uncovered $300K in employee theft, previously unknown to the Company, which potentially avoided a $6.2 million total loss if not for early detection and attention to detail.
- Suggested adoption of three new innovative HR approaches to improve employee engagement, two of which were immediately adopted. Results contributed to a 23% improvement in organization-wide survey results.
- Influenced the division's top HR vendor to change their long-standing service level agreement and to reduce costs of their annual employee benefit administration fees by 17% saving the company $2.6 million.
- Assembled and led a cross-functional team which expanded scope of HR services provided by 25%. This required overcoming resource limitations, departmental conflicts, communication breakdowns and gaining approval from the company's Executive Committee.
- Improved the employee retention rate in the investment services group from 85% to 96% by leading the unique program called *"Beyond The Bottom Line."* This program

and approach has been subsequently adopted by all six regional offices.

Way #5:
USE COMPARISONS

I'm sure you've heard the phrase "it's apples to oranges—you just can't compare the two." Well, on your resume, you CAN if it helps make your point. Comparisons can help you convey that you can run faster, jump higher and leap tall buildings in a single bound better than the next candidate. For instance, this impact statement tells only half the story.

> *Before:*
> - Led initiatives that contributed to a #1 ranking in employee engagement for the Cedar Rapids manufacturing site.

A comparison with some elaboration can convey much more.

> *After:*
> - As the site's HR leader, led initiatives that improved employee engagement by 12 percentage points and increased the site's ranking from #12 to #1 among the 16 food manufacturing locations.

In this case, the addition of the words "As the site's HR leader" gives the reader a much clearer picture of your role in this accomplishment. And, by telling your reader there are 16 sites total, your increase from #12 becomes much more impressive.

Here's another example

> *Before*
> - Selected as the HR leader for the national team that merged 4 fragmented customer service centers into one, single centralized unit.

Compare it with this *After* version, which contains more information on the impact of the accomplishment.

After
- Selected as the HR leader for the national team that merged 4 fragmented customer service centers into one, single centralized unit -- which improved company-wide incoming order-processing time 40%, *the fastest time in the industry.*

In the after version, in addition to the insertion of a specific percentage reduction result, I added a comparison to help clarify the impact of the reductions in lead time. These types of comparisons can convey your value very persuasively to prospective employers.

Other comparisons you might make include the following.

Comparisons between competitors:
...reduced absenteeism from 20% to 8%, currently the lowest among all companies in the consumer retail sector.

Comparisons within the industry:
...improved diversity of Asian women in IT leadership roles by 42%, well above the industry average of 17%.

Comparisons within the company:
...improved manager satisfaction with HR by 13%, the largest annual increase for any HR group in the company's 12-year survey history.

Way #6
EMPHASIZE FAST-TRACK PROMOTIONS
AND RAPID CAREER MOVEMENT

If you've been employed in one organization for a significant period of time, one of the best ways of presenting yourself compellingly is to highlight how quickly you've progressed through various key positions.

As an example, below is a 7-year snapshot of this candidate's work experience. Note how the contributions have been consolidated and quantified to illustrate a series of rapid promotions...

Exhibit 7-1: How To Emphasize Rapid Career Movement

PROFESSIONAL EXPERIENCE

NETFLIX, INC. Los Gatos, CA *[Year] to Present*
$12 billion subscription service provider of streaming movies and TV episodes.

Vice President -- Employee Benefits, Prime Division *[Year] – Present*
Sr. Director – Compensation, Benefits, Payroll & HRIS *[Year] – [Year]*
Director - Benefits, Payroll & HRIS *[Year] – [Year]*
Manager - Compensation & Benefits *[Year] – [Year]*
Compensation Analyst *[Year] – [Year]*

Promoted rapidly through a series of increasingly responsible positions to current role as Vice President of Employee Benefits for Prime Services supporting 2,500 employees. Credited with building a **nationally-recognized, best-in-class benefits function** that has enabled the organization to lower benefit costs per employee every year for last three years -- while retaining top performers.

- Led effort to harmonize benefit programs and change actuarial services resulting in $6.2 million in annualized savings.
- Increased 401(k) plan enrollments by 9.75% with positive employee feedback through aggressive employee education efforts.
- Drove initiative to provide individualized reports which contributed to a turnover reduction from 11% to 4% in customer service centers.
- Reduced healthcare costs by $2.2 million by adding two higher deductible plan options.
- Recruited and developed a talented team of 11 professionals who now serve as Netflix's core employee benefits staff.

Way #7:
USE THE CAR TECHNIQUE
(Challenge, Action & Result)

CAR is a vehicle (pardon the pun) that you use to emphasize the *Challenge* of each of your positions, the *Action* you took, and the *Results* you delivered.

Below is an example of this technique taken from the Fredricks resume in Chapter 11.

Exhibit 7-2: CAR Technique for Presenting Your Experience

PROFESSIONAL EXPERIENCE

WIP SYSTEMS INTERNATIONAL, Waukegan, IL
Director - Human Resources [Year] to [Year]
Director – Organization Development [Year] to [Year]

Challenge: Provide HR leadership for the largest division of this rapidly growing microchip company supporting $600 million in sales, 1700 employees, 7 manufacturing sites, 9 sales forces and 85 HQ personnel in marketing, finance and administration.

Action: Upon promotion to head all HR, developed and executed a comprehensive organization development and labor relations agenda that supported the growth in business performance and elimination of non-performing businesses.

Results:
- **Helped implement large-scale organization change** which consolidated 6 North American supply chain organizations into one single organization -- generating $12.5 million in cost savings. Served as HR leader on the executive design team.
- **Championed execution of talent optimization strategy** which cut key position turnover by 30%, improved leadership bench strength by 20% and increased diversity in leadership roles by 25%.
- **Developed innovative incentive compensation programs** which supported the introduction of a new crucial new product resulting in $25 million in sales above plan.
- **Improved retention of key people by 32%** over prior year's total through customized individual development planning and mentoring for our 16 highest potential managers.

This technique works especially well if you are transitioning from one industry to another because it focuses the reader's attention on your results rather than on the industry in which you delivered them.

You can also use the CAR technique in place of the brief job overview and contribution statements under your professional experience. When doing so, make sure you are consistent in using the identical CAR format for each of your past employers. This conveys consistency and the appearance of a strong, long-term history for taking on challenges and delivering results.

Keep in mind that the CAR presentation technique consumes lots of space. So, if you're trying to keep your resume to one page, avoid it and use a more conventional layout of your job and accomplishments.

Finally, when using CAR, feel free to substitute words that better fit your situation. The word *solution* can be substituted for *action.* You can also substitute other synonyms for *results,* such as *outcomes, contributions* or *impact.*

WHERE TO DIG UP CONTENT FOR YOUR CONTRIBUTIONS AND IMPACT STATEMENTS

By far the best place to find information for your contributions and impact statements is your own *career file* (CF). Every HR professional should have a growing CF, so if you can't lay claim to one now, grab the nearest manila file folder or 9-by-12 envelope and label it "How I've Made a Difference." You can also create a folder in your My Documents folder on your computer. Consider tossing the following items into your CF:

- Attaboys (or "attagirls") from the boss.
- Memos documenting your contributions to a team effort.
- Positive feedback from clients.
- Notes from meetings with your supervisors that state what's expected of you or how your performance will be measured.
- Notes (handwritten is okay) which substantiate that you met or exceeded what was expected of you.
- Notes (with detailed names, facts and figures) of what you consider to be your greatest contributions.
- Company data summaries relevant to your position (quarterly turnover numbers, employee productivity indices, costs, expense controls, etc.). Remember to keep proprietary information confidential.
- Job descriptions.
- Performance evaluations.
- Examples of work you've produced (such as a company brochure or a new business form).

From this raw material, you can compose powerful, substantiated and impressive impact statements that will give you entree to better jobs, outfit you with ammunition that you *are* making a difference in the health of the company and in other people's lives. Next time you have a bad day at the office, take out your career management file and take note of what you have accomplished.

TAKING CREDIT FOR TEAM RESULTS WITHOUT BEING AN ARROGANT JERK

In describing your contributions, it's easy to sound like you "did-it-all-by-yourself." And that flies in the face of today's business climate that values collaboration and teamwork.

So, to avoid this perception of being the Lone Ranger, I commonly see many HR pros make the mistake of entirely omitting an accomplishment if they weren't 100 percent responsible for it.

Avoid this trap. Don't be afraid to list contributions that were accomplished as a member of a team. If you are concerned about taking credit for something that was a collaborative effort, there's a simple answer to your dilemma. Simply begin your impact statement with phrasing such as the following:

> *Contributed to...*
> *Aided in...*
> *Helped to...*
> *Member of 7-person task force that...*
> *Collaborated with department managers to...*
> *Participated on ABC Committee that...*
> *Supported a...*
> *Company-wide efforts led to...*
> *Departmental efforts led to...*
> *Selected for national team that...*

Douglas, a vice president for organization and talent development, used the following statement to share the recognition for a collective accomplishment:

> Core leadership team member that helped implement a *new company-wide online performance management system...* covering all 14,500 employees...that contributed to attaining the company's 12% annual growth objective.

By using the phrase "core management team member," Doug gives credit where credit is due without exaggerating his role. When you get right down to it, you can argue that *any* HR-related accomplishment is really a team accomplishment. Clearly, most HR professionals don't achieve any meaningful results without collaboration with their colleagues, clients or their boss.

The rule of thumb is to give credit to the team if it was a joint effort, but don't hesitate to claim ownership if YOU were the one to envision, initiate, or take the leadership role in the effort. If it's the latter, and it would be politically savvy of you to give credit to the team you headed up (especially when applying for in-house promotions), try one of these suggestions:

Led task force in...
Assembled 7-person task force that...
Chaired ABC Committee that...
Co-led sales campaign that...
Department team leader who...
Orchestrated cross-functional teams in accomplishing...
Directed collaborative efforts that realized...
Headed up national team that...

In resume writing, you walk a fine-line between self-adulation and self-effacement. Too much of the former, and you'll come across as arrogant. Too much of the latter, and you'll look weak. If you're unsure, err on the side of dialing down your role a tick, because reference checks that reveal your resume to be inflated will be grounds for discontinuing your candidacy.

You can always elaborate on your contributions in an interview, and you'll probably score even more points when your explanations reveal that you did more than what was contained on your resume.

However, if you're unsure about this, have an HR-savvy colleague review your impact statements and get his or her read on whether you're giving yourself enough credit.

10 MORE **CRITICAL** TIPS FOR ENHANCING DESCRIPTIONS OF YOUR WORK EXPERIENCE

#1: If you've been out of work for more than 3 months, or have been between jobs more than twice, consider using just the years (e.g. 2013) and omit the months (e.g. May 2013) when listing your jobs. Be aware that hiring authorities may draw negative conclusions when you do this and you run the risk of being passed over. But this is less risky than putting down specific dates that are more likely to call attention to an employment gap and get you eliminated from consideration.

#2: If you have changed jobs within the same firm, don't list every single job separately...as it can look as though you've changed companies. Often, resume readers simply look at your dates of employment – and if they see a one-year stint followed by another year's stint, followed by yet another one-year stint, they may consider you as having had too many jobs. So, if you've had a number of promotions or different jobs with the same company, to clarify this put the comprehensive date *next to the company name.* Then, you can list the dates next to each position within the company, detailing the titles or duties.

#3: When putting an employer's name on resume, if it isn't easily recognized, also state what they do. Some examples:

CONTRIX, Inc. - Fourth largest micro-computing company based in North America with $3.5 billion in sales and 14,000 employees worldwide.

ORGANOVO HOLDINGS, INC. -- $1 billion developer of three-dimensional (3D) printing technology used in hospitals and medical facilities. 7,200 U.S. employees.

If you work for a company whose business is not extremely well known, many resume readers will dismiss your resume simply because they aren't familiar with the company.

Even if you worked for a large, well-recognized organization, it doesn't hurt to name and briefly describe the division as well. For example, stating that you worked for Procter & Gamble *only* is not as effective as including *also* that you were in P&G's Laundry Detergents Group or Prescription Drug Division. This helps clarify and ensures that the person reading the resume understands what that company's business entails and the specific environment you worked in.

#4: Make sure your titles are not confusing. Titles can screen you out of the selection process. Witty or creative titles in HR currently seem to be all the rage these days at new start-ups or in some high tech organizations. If it's not clear from the title exactly what you did, change it to a more conventional title people will recognize more readily. If you have a nutty or oddball title and, for whatever reason, you feel you must use it, put it in parentheses, next to the traditional title.

For example, if your unusual title of People Advocate is actually the same as an HR Manager elsewhere, you might want to display it as:

> **XYZ TECHNOLOGIES**
> HR Manager ("People Advocate") *[Year] - [Year]*

However, you be the judge. Remember subsequent reference checking will likely surface your actual job title, so you may want to avoid dropping it entirely.

#5: Create attention-grabbing sentences. For more powerful sentences for the contributions and impact statements you've listed under each job, here are some key points to follow:

- I know this is obvious, but it deserves mentioning. Don't use personal pronouns (I, my, me). Instead of saying: *"I planned, organized, and directed the timely and accurate*

*production of code products with estimated annual reve-
nues of $1 million"* you should say: *"Planned, organized,
and directed.. "* Your reader assumes you are referring to
yourself, so personal pronouns can be avoided.

- Use action verbs at the beginning of each sentence (*designed, supervised, managed, developed, formulated, and
so on*) to make them more powerful.
- Incorporate keywords for the specific HR job you're targeting.

Applying the above, below are examples of re-written sentences
that were on real resumes. Note the use of action verbs at the
beginning of each sentence and use of *italicized* keywords.

Original Sentence:

Responsible for leading team of *organization development*
consultants, management trainers and software designers.

Rewrite:

Led a team of 20 *organization development* consultants,
management trainers and software designers in delivering
online customized leadership training to clients

Original Sentence:

Inside *recruiting and staffing* support for the aftermarket
equipment division. Responsible for filling 60 jobs in 13
states in 27 days which set a company record.

Rewrite:

Provided *recruiting and staffing* support for the aftermarket
equipment division. Filled 60 jobs in 13 states in 27 days --
a company record.

#6: In general, devote more resume space to your recent jobs, especially ones that are more applicable to the position you are applying for. However, if you've been in your current position for only one year and have spent fifteen years in your previous position, hiring authorities will likely be more interested in the previous fifteen years than in your past year. The longer you have worked in an organization and the more recent your experience, the more detail you need to provide.

#7: Prioritize your experience under each job with the most important descriptions first. Think logically and from the perspective of a potential employer. Keep related items together so the reader does not jump from one concept to another. Make the thoughts flow smoothly.

#8: Pick 2-4 accomplishments for each job title and edit them down to bite-size chunks that read like a classified ad. Write as if you had to pay for each entry by the word. This approach can help you pack a lot of information into a short space. The resulting abbreviated style will help convey a sense of immediacy to the reader.

Some examples:

- Initiated major employee benefit cost reductions of $3.2 million in the first year while gaining employee buy-in.
- Earned the *HR Gold Medal Award* for three consecutive years for success in driving employee engagement at XYZ Company.
- Improved the sales training utilization rate from 55% to 81% which contributed to record revenues for the Southern Region.

Now, while you may tell the reader about these achievements, *never detail how they were accomplished*; the key phrase here is **"specifically vague."** The intent of your resume is to pique interest and to raise as many questions as you answer. Questions mean interest, interest means talking to you, and *getting conversations started is the primary goal of your resume.*

#9: The following guidelines might be of help in determining how many impact statements to use and where to position them:

- **When the bulk of your experience is with your most recent employer:** If you've worked for your present or most recent employer for a number of years or for the bulk of your career (and this experience is relevant to what you want to do next), you'll want to give the most weight, and provide the most impact statements, to this employer. Seven to eight impact statements might well be in order if this is the case.

- **When your employment history is evenly distributed among employers:** If your employment history has been fairly consistent in length of time spent with employers, use a similar number of impact statements for each employer, perhaps two to four for each. Give slightly more weight to the most recent employer, perhaps three or five impact statements total or one or two more than you allot to the remainder of your employers.

- **When you have been employed with your most recent company for a short period of time:** If it's too soon to have made a measurable difference at your current employer, refrain from including an impact statement because a weak statement is less impressive than no statement at all. Likewise, be brief with your job description for this employer and begin with wording which implies that you are currently tackling some new challenge. Use, for instance, *Currently charged with...* or *Challenged with...* or *Recruited to....*

- **Finally, there's no hard and fast rule about the "right" number of impact statements to use.** In general, the further back in your career the job was, the fewer impact statements you'll use. When space is a consideration, eliminate impact statements from the earliest experience (you'll see this frequently in many of the examples in Chapter 11). Don't feel that because you included impact statements under the most recent employers, you must include them also under the most dated employers. You have a great deal of flexibility in what information you include.

#10: Think in threes. Psychologically, the mind likes groups of three. Whether making decisions about format, the number of items to include in a list, or the items in a sentence…consider using threes to group your thoughts. This is a loose guideline and you need not apply it religiously in 100 percent of cases. Don't think that you can never again write a sentence that contains a list of two items or four items. Just be aware that groups of three often balance best.

That does it for rules, guidelines and tips for selling your Professional Experience to recruiters and hiring authorities. Let's now move on to the Formal Education section of your resume.

8

Rule Four:
ADD PUNCH & IMPACT TO YOUR FORMAL EDUCATION

The Education section of your resume should include degrees, certifications, credentials and continuing education.

If any are particularly notable, be sure to highlight them prominently in your Education section or bring them to the top and include them in your Summary (see the Nina Washington resume in Chapter 11).

You should also be aware of the unwritten "three-year rule." There is an implied three-year guideline for determining where to position your education.

- **Place your education toward the bottom of the resume** and below your experience if you graduated more than three years ago and gained relevant experience in the meantime. If decades have passed since you finished college, definitely place education at the bottom of the resume and eliminate dates of graduation.
- **Place education near the top of your resume** if you received a degree within the past three years and the degree is related to the role you're seeking.
- **This three year rule also applies to listing your GPA.** I recommend that you list your GPA if you are a recent

graduate (three years out of school or less) where your resume will be competing against those of fellow students in your college's electronic resume database. **However, only list it if it's a terrific GPA.** Otherwise, leave it off. What's terrific? A GPA of 3.5 or above, clearly. If yours is 3.0 to 3.5, it neither helps nor hurts you, in most cases. Anything from 2.9 or below can actually hurt your chances of getting an interview, in which case I'd recommend dropping it.

With the above in mind, the following examples illustrate a variety of ways to organize and format your Education section

Format for Highlighting Your Executive Education

EDUCATION

Executive Development Program
   STANFORD UNIVERSITY
Advanced Management Program in Human Resources
   UNIVERSITY OF MICHIGAN
Masters of Business Administration (MBA) Degree
   PURDUE UNIVERSITY
Bachelor of Science (BS) Degree
   ILLINOIS STATE UNIVERSITY

Format for Emphasizing Your HR Certifications

EDUCATION & CERTIFICATIONS

Bachelor of Science (BS)
   University of Virginia, Charlottesville, VA
Senior Professional in Human Resources (SPHR)
   Society for Human Resources Management
Certified Compensation Professional (CCP)
   World at Work

Format for Describing Continuing Professional Development

EDUCATION

M.S. Organization Development
Georgia State University, *[Year]*
B.S. Biology
Texas A&M University, *[Year]*

Highlights of Continuing Professional Education:
- Organizational Management & Leadership, California Leadership Association, *[Year]*
- Conflict Resolution & Violence Management in the Workplace, Institute for Workplace Safety, *[Year]*.
- Maintaining Non-Union Status, Wisconsin Management Institute, *[Year]*.

Educational Format for the Recent College Grad

EDUCATION

BACHELOR OF SCIENCE, Psychology, May, *[Year]*
Howard University, Washington, D.C.
Graduated Magna Cum Laude (GPA: 3.95)

HR relevant course work completed: Organizational Psychology, Talent Management, HR Management & Metrics, Organization Development, Employment Law.
- **Minor in International Business:** Introduction to World Cultures, International Politics, International Economics.
- **Selected for the special *Human Factors Leadership Course*** that provided hands-on experience in the use of modeling technology to predict impact of employee performance on business results.
- **Honors:** Golden Key National Scholar, National Honor Society, President of Campus United Way Organization.

For recent college grads: As indicated in the previous example, go heavy on the Education section. If you've had little/no HR-related experience, your education is your strongest selling point. So don't be afraid to really sell it and let it take up "prime shelf space"—that is at the visual center at the **top of the page** of your resume.

Format for a Degree Clearly Unrelated to HR

EDUCATION

Bachelor of Arts (B.A.) Degree, RICE UNIVERSITY.
Houston, Texas

When your degree is viewed as unrelated to either HR or business and you are competing against individuals with these types of degrees, consider listing just the degree and eliminate the major. Place both the degree and the college on one line to "thicken" the line and camouflage the fact that you haven't listed the major. In the example above, Irene held a 3-year-old degree in Music from Rice and was applying for a position as Manager of Talent Acquisition, for which she had an excellent background. She successfully used this approach.

Note: This strategy of dropping the major is <u>NOT</u> a hard-and-fast rule. In some cases, a major apart from the HR profession can make you even more interesting as a candidate, especially if you have pursued related training since graduating from college. Obviously, it's your call.

Various Formats for Those Without Degrees

EDUCATION

SAN DIEGO STATE UNIVERSITY, San Diego, CA
Dual Majors in Management & Human Resources Administration (2 years completed)

TRAINING & EDUCATION

BACHELOR OF SCIENCE, MANAGEMENT
Hawaii Pacific University, Honolulu, Hawaii
- Five classes short of completing an undergraduate degree
- Selected for the Dean's List
- Relevant course work completed: Industrial/Organizational Psychology, Talent Management, HR Management & Metrics, Organization Development, Employment Law.

EDUCATION

BAYLOR UNIVERSITY, Waco, TX (Year – Year)
BS Candidate -- Business Administration
(Senior class status)

EDUCATION

SAN DIEGO STATE UNIVERSITY, San Diego, CA
Dual Majors in Management & Human Resources Administration (2 years completed)

Many people have sincere intentions and plans to finish college, but life sometimes gets in the way. For those who've completed most of a degree but didn't take home a sheepskin, consider one of the above alternatives.

Whichever method you choose, just make sure it is quite clear that you didn't graduate. Obviously, falsifying education and training on a resume is a no-no.

Format When The School Outranks The Degree

EDUCATION

STANFORD UNIVERSITY, Palo Alto, CA
Bachelor of Arts, Psychology *[Year]*
- Graduated summa cum laude.
- Vice President, Student Council

In the above example, if your university is widely recognized as being among the top universities in the country, capitalize on it...especially if it's *perceived* to carry more weight than your degree. If this is the case, list it first so the reader focuses on the school.

Format When Degree Outranks the School

EDUCATION

MASTER OF BUSINESS ADMINISTRATION (MBA)
Concentration: Finance and Human Resources, *[Year]*
Florida Atlantic University, Boca Raton, FL
- President, National MBA Association
- Recipient of the Outstanding FAU Student Award for outstanding leadership & academic achievement *[Year]*.

If your degree is *perceived* to be more prestigious than the university where it was earned, list your education with the degree first. (No offense, FAU!).

Format For Extraordinary Success
Beyond-The-Classroom

If you're a recent graduate with a B.S. degree seeking an HR role, the competition is intense. If you've attained outstanding success beyond the classroom, this is the time play it up. In the following example, note how the candidate used her education

---

section to also elaborate on her outstanding athletic and leadership accomplishments:

<u>EDUCATION</u>

NOTRE DAME UNIVERSITY, South Bend, IN
B.S. Organization Psychology, *[Year]*
- 4-year Notre Dame Basketball Varsity Letterman and Senior Captain at Forward
- Awarded Capital One Academic All-American honors for Women's Basketball and recognized for "Scholarship, leadership, performance & dedication to the Notre Dame athletics program."
- Captained the team that reached the NCAA Championship quarter-finals in *[Year]*.

Details, Details, Details
The devil's in the details and tiny resume details really do matter. Something as simple as a date in your education can affect whether your resume will land you an interview. For instance, writing from-to dates (2010-2013) implies that you did not graduate. If you graduated with a degree, list only the year you graduated (2009) or the month and year (May, 2014) if you're a recent grad. Computerized applicant tracking systems and Internet resume databases are programmed to show that you have college study but not a degree if they see "from-to" dates.

Accredited Colleges and Universities
One last cautionary note on your education: Most companies and all government organizations require that your degree come from a regionally accredited college or university. If you have a degree from a diploma mill, it will not be accepted and should not be listed on your resume. To determine whether your school is regionally accredited, check with the Council for Higher Education Accreditation at www.chea.org/directories/regional.asp.

9

Rule Five:
USE RESUME BOOSTERS TO
SET YOURSELF APART
FROM YOUR COMPETITION

We've covered the core elements of your resume. However, there are some other categories and enhancements you'll want to consider including on your resume, depending on your experience and your current objectives.

One caution: apply these additional elements *selectively.* You don't want to clutter up your resume with so much crap that it detracts from your major contributions.

Resume Booster #1:
SHOWCASE YOUR GLOBAL PERSPECTIVE

In today's global economy, any international exposure or experience you've had here is a differentiator. Formal HR-related experience outside of the U.S. is high demand. If you speak a foreign language, that's a big plus too.

Even if you've done none of these things, showing evidence that you studied abroad, completed a foreign exchange program or worked successful with businesses in other countries (e.g.

Brazil, Russia, India, China, etc), can be a competitive edge for you with organizations with locations spread around the world.

Here are some examples of how you might highlight this:

Key Contributions:
- Partnered with colleagues in China and India to standardize the current performance evaluation and career development programs as part of the company's 20-country global rollout.

Key Contributions:
- Used personal knowledge of Spanish and Russian to assist the global HR executives in translating 65 HR policies for implementation in Europe and Asia.

EDUCATION

University of Barcelona, Barcelona, Spain *(Spring, Year)*
Studied abroad: 12 hours of classroom study integrated with field experiences in Spain, France and the UK. .

Resume Booster #2:
DROP NAMES

If you've worked with well-known people, name names. Feature them on your resume. But include enough information so that the reader will know their importance.

Example:

Key Contributions:
- Was selected by PepsiCo's CEO, Indra Nooyi (#2 on the Fortune's List of the World's Most Powerful Women) to serve on a committee that successfully streamlined the company's succession planning process by 2 weeks.

In addition to mentioning the names of key individuals, you should also mention the names of prominent firms, customers, strategic partners, vendors or consultants you've dealt with.

Example:

Key Contributions:
- During the corporate downsizing, worked with directly with HR executives at Google, Kraft, and Pfizer to redeploy 12 Finance managers which saved $1.25 million in outplacement expenses.

Resume Booster #3:
USE ENDORSEMENTS

Endorsements can beef up your candidacy in situations where you lack certain qualifications or are competing against more experienced candidates. For examples, go view the resumes of Jill Martinez and Mary Bates in Chapter 11.
- In Martinez' case she uses endorsements to offset her inexperience and has tailored her resume accordingly.
- In Bates' case she's using them to add more punch to her qualifications, given that she lacks a college degree.

When using this tactic, select your endorsers carefully. Use no more than two and make sure they're well-respected industry leaders at a senior-executive level. If you can't get testimonials from these types of individuals, don't include any at all.

Special Note: Even if you don't use endorsements on your resume, include plenty of them (at least 5-8) on your **LinkedIn profile.** This is a wise back-up strategy because if your resume makes the cut, your profile will certainly be checked.

Resume Booster #4:
PLAY UP YOUR AWARDS & HONORS

If you've won prominent honors and awards, include them in a separate section on your resume or as part of the Education or

Experience section, whichever is most appropriate. If you include them in a separate section, here's an example format:

AWARDS & HONORS

Golden Eagle Award for HR Leadership
For Innovations in Attracting Talent, *(Year)*
Human Resources Professional of the Year
Miami Human Resources Association, *(Year)*
Summa Cum Laude Graduate
Columbia University, *(Year)*

Finally, here's a trick for presenting accomplishments when there's a gap of several years since winning any special award.

AWARDS & HONORS

Impressive 5-year record of corporate, national and regional HR honors, including:

- **Chairman's Award for HR Excellence** (won twice) for outstanding results in driving employee engagement.
- **SHRM's Human Capital Leadership Award,** Winner for West Coast Region.
- **Top Forty Under 40 in Business** recognized by Sacramento Business Journal.
- **United Way's "Above & Beyond Award"** for Corporate Fundraising Leadership.
- **HR Impact Award Finalist,** Society for Industrial & Organization Psychology (SIOP).

Resume Booster #5
INCLUDE MEANINGFUL COUNCILS, PROJECT TEAMS, COMMITTEES & TASK FORCES

Most HR leaders and executives serve on councils, committees, task forces and other special project teams either as part of, or in addition to, their full-time responsibilities. This type of information further strengthens your credibility, qualifications and perceived value to prospective employers. Here's a format you might use to present that information:

- **Chairperson,** Committee on Developing Human Resources Talent, *[Year - Year]*

- **Member,** Corporate Council for Maximizing Employee Productivity, *[Year - Year]*

- **Member,** HRIS, Social Media & New Technology Task Force, *[Year - Year]*

- **Project Leader**, Study Team on Human Resources Best Practices, *[Year - Year]*

Resume Booster #6:
HIGHLIGHT YOUR TRAINING
& TEACHING EXPERIENCE

Many HR pros also teach or train at local colleges, universities and other organizations in addition to training that they do as part of their day job. If you have this type of experience, here's an example of how you might present this information:

- **Adjunct Faculty,** Department of Business, Loyola University. Teaching "Introduction to Talent Management" to third- and fourth-year students. *[Year - Present]*

- **Guest Lecturer,** Department of Business & Economics, University of Illinois. Providing semi-annual, weekend lecture series on the role of diversity and inclusion in today's corporate workplace, *[Year - Present]*.

- **Lecturer,** Department of Business Administration, Calumet College. Taught "Principles of Human Resources" to second-year college students. *[Year - Year]*

Including this experience communicates a strong message about your leadership, expertise and communications skills.

However, **relevant** is a key word here. Always look at your resume from the perspective of a potential employer. Don't waste space by listing training that is not directly or indirectly related to your target job.

Resume Booster #7:
CONSIDER YOUR PUBLIC PRESENTATIONS

One of the best ways of demonstrating your expertise is through public presentations at conferences, seminars, workshops and training programs.

So if you've had public speaking experience, others must consider you an expert. And this represents yet another opportunity to elevate you from the pack.

In the example below, the candidate demonstrates her specialized Human Resources expertise in working with Information Technology (IT) leaders, clients and organizations...

- Keynote Speaker, *"Strategies for Attracting IT Talent,"* The American Association for IT Professionals (AAITP) Regional Conference, Chicago, IL *[Year]*

- Session Leader, *"Creating A High-Performance Culture for IT Professionals,"* Organization Development Network, Glenview, IL [Year]

- Panel Presenter, *"Staffing The IT Organization For Success,"* The Society for Human Resources Management (SHRM) National Meeting, San Diego, CA *[Year]*

- Keynote Speaker, *"Retaining IT Talent During Turbulent Times,"* National Association of African-Americans in Human Resources (NAAHR), Chicago, IL *[Year]*

Resume Booster #8:
ARE YOU PUBLISHED?

Similar to delivering public presentations, if you're published, others will perceive you as an expert. Demonstrating your expertise in print validates your knowledge, qualifications and credibility. Publications can include books, articles, blogs, online website content, manuals and other written documents.

An example:

- Author, *"Hiring High-Potentials For Long Term Retention,"* Society of Human Resources Management Annual Conference Proceedings, *[Year]*.

- Author, *"How Top Companies Are Assessing Their High Potential Talent,"* Consulting Psychology Journal: Practice and Research, *[Month, Year]*.

- Author, *"The Pearls and Perils of Identifying Employee Potential,"* Industrial and Organizational Psychology: Annual Perspectives on Science and Practice, *[Year]*.

- Co-Author, *"The New Promise of Performance Management During Volatile Times,"* Motorola Employee Bulletin, *[Month, Year]*

Resume Booster #9:
DON'T DISCOUNT YOUR
PROFESSIONAL AFFILIATIONS

If you're a member of any HR, professional or leadership association, consider including that information on your resume. It conveys a message of professionalism, a desire to stay current with the industry and a strong professional network. If you've held leadership positions within these organizations, be sure to stress that as well.

Example:

DETROIT AREA HUMAN RESOURCES ASSOCIATION
Vice-President *(Year - Present)*
Program Development Committee Chair *(Year - Year)*
Recruitment Committee Member *(Year - Year)*

If you are no longer a member of some organizations but want to include them for impact, add the words "Past and Present" after the Affiliations heading...and then place the more dated affiliations at the bottom of the list. Many candidates use this strategy to weave in older affiliations that supported their candidacy.

In the example below, note how it allows inclusion of past leadership experiences in the last two listings.

AFFILIATIONS -- PAST AND PRESENT

- Organization Development Network (ODN) - Region 12 Professional Development Committee

- American Society for Training & Development (ASTD) - Member

- Sioux City Human Resources Association - Past President

- Central Valley Language Arts Council—Past President

Finally, avoid using abbreviations (e.g. SDHRA as a substitute for San Diego Human Resources Association). Don't assume the reader will know what such acronyms mean. If it's worth including on your resume, it's worth spelling out.

Resume Booster #10:
COMBINE CATEGORIES

You may face a situation where you have so many additional categories at the end of your resume, each with only a few lines, that spacing becomes a problem. Or perhaps you have a few small bits of information that you think are important but don't merit an entire section. In either of these cases, consider consolidating the information using a single heading such as "Professional Achievements," "Professional Profile" or "Professional Leadership." See the example below for a Compensation professional:

PROFESSIONAL ACHIEVEMENTS

Education
Juris Doctor, Kent College of Law, Chicago, IL
Bachelor of Arts, Indiana University, Bloomington, IN

Leadership Committees
World at Work Association, Vice-President
Human Resources Planning Society, Program Committee
United Way, Co-Chair

Public Speaking
New Compensation Strategy Forum, Phoenix, *[Year]*
World at Work National Meeting, New York, *[Year]*
Panelist, Compensation Association Planning Meeting, Chicago, *[Year]*

Language Proficiencies
Fluent in English, Spanish and French

Note how this allows you to save a bit of resume space while emphasizing individual items with their own category headings.

Remember, the above sections are normally at the bottom of your resume. However, if this information is especially significant – that is, you won a prestigious award, spoke at an international conference or wrote an article for a respected HR, business or related publication -- you might not want to hide it at the end, but instead include it at the top of your resume as part of your Summary section. Again, your Summary is designed to be the grabber, the differentiator and command attention.

Resume Booster #11:
ATTACH "SUCCESS" DOCUMENTS

One candidate I hired into an HR Director's role attached two summary pages to his resume showing he scored in the 92nd percentile (upper 8 percent) of the management population on his firm's mandatory 360' survey. After checking my sources to confirm his results and getting more detail from him, this certainly worked in his favor. He later told me he'd gotten quite a few interviews because of this add-on to his resume.

Success attachments are designed to further substantiate your success and should be relatively <u>short</u> and <u>obvious.</u> At a glance they should communicate, "My resume and cover letter state that I am a very successful HR professional -- and here's proof."

What kind of information does this comprise? It could include:

- Past positive performance reviews.
- Exceedingly positive recent 360' feedback results.
- Personal psychological evaluations that show high rankings in leadership.
- News releases of recognition and honors; or
- Any objective document that substantiates your success, as long as it is concise and clear when viewed.

Often you'll find that these attachments get viewed *before* the resume itself is read.

Anything that separates you from the average candidate can be attached -- again along as it's no more than a couple of pages, provides a summary of a successful achievement and isn't a gimmick. Anything more than this will get tossed.

The strategies in this Chapter are designed to boost the impact of your resume. However, all will not be applicable. So be highly selective of those you choose to include.

10

Rule Six:
MAKE SURE IT CAN PASS THE
15-SECOND SCAN TEST

Recruiters are the most overworked creatures walking the planet.
Most times, they may be working to fill as many as 20-30 different positions at the same time…some in HR, some not…and also
quick scanning over 40-50 resumes (or more) for each of those
jobs. And even though it's likely they're in HR just like you, they
may not have in-depth understanding of the specific HR role
you're applying for.

So your resume has about 15 seconds to really impress him or
her or it will be set aside, probably forever.

Here are some strategies for passing their initial scan test and
holding their attention for a just a *little…bit…longe*r…

Use the EXACT job title
When applying for a specific position, it's important that the job
title is easily identifiable on your resume. And there's no better
way to ensure that than to put it plainly at the top of the document. This gives the manager the information he or she needs to
know—exactly the position you want. For examples, see the
Martinez and Johnson resumes in Chapter 11.

This is also an area on your resume that's easily customizable as you apply for specific jobs at different organizations. Hint, hint...change it as you apply for specific positions.

Capture your unique value in a one-line statement
The best companies use slogans to communicate value to their potential clients. For example, Subway's current motto is *"Eat Fresh."* That sums it up. Plenty of hungry consumers choose Subway over other fast food joints as a means to more healthful eating. Follow their lead. Create a one-line statement that sums up the expertise, benefit, or value you offer a potential employer, and put that in your Summary. For an example, in McFee's resume in Chapter 11, you'll see she's positioned herself as an *HR Leader with General Management and P&L Experience.* With this statement, she stands as a rare bird among other HR candidates, most of whom have not had experience running a business with full profit and loss accountability.

Load your keywords into your Summary
It will focus the reviewer on those words that he or she regards as most relevant and aligned to their search.

Put your best stuff above the fold
Don't hide your most compelling credentials. Your most impressive selling points and your most notable successes and impact statements should be placed in the top third of your resume. You don't want to bury details that could make you the best choice. This applies to your second page as well. So make sure you start the top of page 2 with something important.

One last piece of advice on maximizing the first third of your resume -- **include a link to your LinkedIn profile** within the contact information at the top of your resume. This way, once you ace that initial 15-second resume scan—and they're really chomping at the bit for more information about you—they'll have easy access to your LinkedIn profile and all the great information you've put there. Hopefully, it will include all those wonderful endorsements and recommendations your colleagues and previous employers have written about you.

Finally, do your own 15-second review.
Pretend you are a recruiter trying to fill a position that you know you're very well suited for. Scan your resume for 15 seconds and circle everything that stands out. Make sure the first line is compelling and your track record stands out.

Then ask yourself:

- Do your accomplishments jump off the page?
- Is your work experience clearly conveyed?
- Do your qualifications pop within those 15 seconds?
- Do your paragraphs act as "speed bumps" that slow you down as you scan through it?

Edit and eliminate fluff
When the fifteen seconds are done, edit your resume to reflect what you learned.

- Slice long paragraphs up into a few crisp, concise, focused bullets that can effectively tell the same story.
- Drop wordy job descriptions that lack factual support.
- Cut fluff, such as "dynamic leader," "excellent communication skills," and "effective listener"
- Make sure each bullet is 2-3 lines at most. Short, powerful bullets give reasons to keep reading.

Then consider showing your new resume to a trusted colleague for their feedback.

For many people, crafting your accomplishments is the hardest part of writing a resume. If you remember nothing else, keep in mind that you should quantify whenever possible. Numbers are always impressive. Finally, don't duplicate wording throughout the resume. If you use dollars in one case, use percentages in another. Overused words lose their effectiveness, like a song played on the radio again and again.

11

20 KILLER HR RESUMES YOU CAN USE AS MODELS FOR YOUR OWN

In this chapter, you'll find out what an irresistible resume looks like. There are 20 resumes here representing a full spectrum of HR professionals from VPs to the new college grad – and just about every specialty within HR. And they all illustrate the strategies described in this book.

All these resumes are real, but I've altered them in some spots to preserve confidentiality. So there's no need for you to struggle or start from scratch! Hopefully, they should guide you in developing your own resume that is uniquely YOU. *Take your time and review ALL them.*

For your convenience, these resumes have been reduced in size so that they all can fit in this book. **However, you can view or download a full, 8½ x 11" version of all of them in all their glory – at this website:**

> **HRResumeSecrets.com/documents2-1168807.htm**

Finally, I'd encourage you to go to page 146 to read up on the story and <u>strategy</u> behind each of these resumes. I'm sure you'll find this helpful as well. Enjoy!

Resume 1: HR Leader With a Specialty

JOSH L. KAMINSKI, J.D.

1234 N. Evergreen Street #123 • Somers, NY • 12345 • (354) 255-5558 • joshk2323@email.com

---

SUMMARY

Forward thinking, legally-trained **Human Resources Leader with an industry-wide reputation** for growing high-performing Sales teams and leaders. Trusted advisor able to win buy-in for major change.

Towering Strengths: Attracting & Retaining Talent, Organization Development, Leading Change.

EXPERIENCE

MasterCard, Purchase, NY – *leading technology company engaged in the global payments industry.*

DIRECTOR -- HUMAN RESOURCES, U.S. NATIONAL SALES *[Year - Present]*
Aggressively recruited to lead a team of 11 HR and Training professionals. Supporting a $1 billion sales organization comprised of 1,800 sales employees. Key contributions:

- **Increased revenue per salesperson** through elimination of the lowest performing 10% of sales reps and replacing them with top performers. Led this effort by providing assessments, coaching and ensuring decisions made were legally-defensible.
- **Cut costs** by executing a robust Sales Employee Referral Program that propelled referrals to 13% of total hires resulting in lower cost-per-hire for sales reps and $325,000 in savings the first year.
- **Improved retention** of high performing sales staff by 12% by partnering with sales managers and winning Division CEO support for 3 key initiatives to "re-recruit" at-risk candidates.
- **Attracted higher quality talent** by positioning the MasterCard Sales Organization as an "Employer of Choice" through enhanced company branding and external marketing efforts.

Netflix, Los Gatos, CA – *leading subscription service provider of movies and TV episodes.*

DIRECTOR – TALENT & ORGANIZATION DEVELOPMENT *[Year – Year]*
Promoted to head leadership development and sales training for over 1,200 sales professionals.

- **Deepened bench strength** for regional sales manager and key executive roles by 25% and 22% respectively through leadership of and aggressive follow-up on the talent review process.
- **Enhanced sales capability** through the creation of a *Sales Leadership Institute* that accelerated internal best practice sharing & imported external "best-in-class" sales practices.

DIRECTOR – SALES TRAINING *[Year - Year]*

- **Improved sales training ROI** by 9.7% by revamping the sales training curriculum, streamlining training registration, increasing training provided online and enhancing cost tracking systems.

Other Related Experiences:
Sr. Human Resources Manager, Spherion Technology *(Year-Year)*
Kaminski & Associates, Private Practice in Employment Law *(Year-Year)*
Employment Attorney, Pizza Hut *(Year - Year)*

EDUCATION & PROFESSIONAL LEADERSHIP

Juris Doctor, Loyola University College of Law, Chicago, IL
Bachelor of Arts, Indiana University, Bloomington, IN

Chair, Professional Development Committee, Organization Development Network – *[Year –Year]*
Keynote Speaker: *"Developing High Performing Sales Organizations"* delivered at The American Association for Sales Professionals (AASP) National Conference, Chicago, IL *[Year]*

Resume 2: One Page HR VP Resume

CYNTHIA B. SILVERSTONE
1234 N. Main Street #123• Miami, Florida • 12345
(555) 555-5558 • cb_silverstone26@email.com

SUMMARY

SENIOR TALENT MANAGEMENT EXECUTIVE skilled at collaborating with executive business leaders in attracting, developing and retaining the talent needed to deliver their business plan. Ten years of demonstrated success in developing low-cost, high-impact global HR strategies that work in the U.S. and emerging markets.

PROFESSIONAL HIGHLIGHTS

New Century Apparel—$600 million global retailer of women's lifestyle apparel with 4,500 employees.

VICE-PRESIDENT – GLOBAL TALENT MANAGEMENT *[Year – Present]*
Corporate officer recruited to build and ensure execution of a comprehensive talent strategy to enable expansion of the business into new markets and categories. Reporting to CEO.

- **Led the talent acquisition strategy** which staffed 35 brand new apparel stores in Latin America with 165 critical managers and key retail personnel – 45 days before store launch – a company record.
- **Partnered with the CEO, CFO and CMO** on customized talent initiatives which:
  -- Re-recruited and improved retention of our top performing Store Managers by 12%.
  -- Reduced Marketing Group overhead expenses and redundancies saving $1.5 million.
  -- Restructured the HR function with no service disruption saving $200,000 annually.
- **Built and co-facilitated annual talent review sessions** with the executive team. Identified the "top 100" high potential leaders available for international assignments and ensured plans in place to make them "promotion-ready" within 18 months. 47% moved into new or expanded assignments.
- **Championed new performance management system** -- covering all 4,500 employees -- aimed at tracking & building employee capabilities aligned with the company's 20% annual growth objective.

Google -- $50 billion technology company focused on ways people connect with information.

DIRECTOR – TALENT ACQUISITION *[Year – Year]*
Sourced, recruited and interviewed candidates for executive, engineering and technical positions.

- **Staffed over 300 software engineering and IT positions** in 11 months with a 24% increase in the candidate acceptance rate.
- **Led the re-design of the new employee orientation process** which cut the critical six-month turnover rate by 26% and saved $1.2 million in recruiting costs.
- **Improved "time to fill" for sales and account executive positions** in Asia from 52 to 27 days on average – through improved association networks and social media relationships.

Other Related Experiences:
Senior Manager – Corporate Staffing & Recruitment, Hewlett-Packard *[Year-Year]*
Senior Manager – Learning & Organization Development, Coca-Cola *[Year-Year]*
Consultant - Human Resource Operations, Verizon *[Year – Year]*

EDUCATION

Stanford Advanced Management Program
B.S. in Business Administration, Texas A&M University

ASSOCIATION LEADERSHIP

Board Diversity Chair, Society of Human Resources Management (SHRM), *[Year] & [Year]*
Employer Advisory Committee, Goodwill Industries, Job Creation Program, *[Year – Year]*

Resume 3: Recent Grad Seeking First Full-Time Position in HR

NINA S. WASHINGTON

1455 Clinton Way • Washington, DC 20059 • ninawash89@earthnet.com • (262) 997-5456

SUMMARY

Recent MBA graduate with concentration in Human Resources.
HR/OD intern experience with two prominent organizations—meeting aggressive deadlines on projects. Proven ability to collaborate with clients and extensive campus leadership experiences.

EDUCATION

MBA – Concentration in Human Resources *[Month, Year]*
Howard University, Washington D.C.
Relevant courses: Organizational Psychology, Talent Management, HR Management & Metrics, Organizational Development, Research and Survey Methods, Employment Law, and Marketing.

BS in MATHEMATICS *[Month, Year]*
Amherst College, Amherst, MA -- Study Abroad Program (Germany)

HUMAN RESOURCES EXPERIENCE

PROCTER & GAMBLE, Cincinnati, OH
Organizational Development Intern *[Month, Year – Month, Year]*
- Administered and managed the employee engagement pulse survey process covering 300 employees in the IT Systems group. Three recommendations for action were implemented.
- Interviewed incumbents and helped develop an Accounting & Finance competency model used to prioritize the development needs of 150 managers and directors in the 2nd largest division.
- Assisted in the development of diversity and inclusion training materials which were later used to train 250 supervisor and middle managers.

MERRILL LYNCH FINANCIAL INC., Charlotte, NC
Human Resource Intern *[Month, Year – Month, Year]*
- Revamped interview questionnaire. Pre-screened 50 potential candidates for nonexempt clerical positions in the Fixed Income and Emerging Markets Equity departments resulting in 10 hires. 100% positive feedback from hiring managers on quality of hires.
- Revised and updated 150 job descriptions and developed preliminary compensation levels and pay recommendations for 35 clerical and administrative jobs.

LEADERSHIP EXPERIENCE

HOWARD MATHEMATICS DEPARTMENT, Washington, DC
Graduate Teaching Assistant *[Month, Year – Month, Year]*
- Taught Introduction to Statistics for freshman classes of 60+ students each semester.
- Graded exams and provided research assistance to Assistant Professor of Mathematics.

ALPHA NU PHI PROFESSIONAL BUSINESS SORORITY
Chair of Fundraising *[Month, Year – Month, Year]*
- Generated $25,000.00 in fundraising revenue from four events over the course of the year.
- Trained 20 new fundraisers. Developed and implemented new marketing strategies which increased individual and faculty contributors by 27%.

GENE & GRACE'S RESTAURANT, Washington, DC *[Month, Year – Month, Year]*
Seasonal Host -- Served as first contact for restaurant customers. Coordinated reservations and seating.

VOLUNTEER EXPERIENCE
Math Tutor for High School Students, Habitat for Humanity, St. Anthony's Food Mission

---

Resume 4: Light on HR Experience, Applying for a Posted Job.

JILL J. MARTINEZ

21455 Nixon Drive • Bay City, MI 10029 • jill_martinez@email.com • (216) 897-3452

CANDIDATE FOR HR ANALYST
INTERNATIONAL DIVISION AT CITIBANK
Summary of Qualifications:

Experience in job placement, recruiting and training.
Intercultural sensitivity, having lived abroad in Europe for two years.
Ability to represent the organization with professionalism and confidence.
Multilingual, fluent in Spanish & French -- written, verbal and in presentations.

EDUCATION

Bachelor of Arts, International Relations/Business, [Year]
Rochester College, Rochester, NY -- Study Abroad Program (Barcelona, Spain)

HUMAN RESOURCES & INTERNATIONAL EXPERIENCE

Career Placement Specialist & Recruiter, STATE OF MICHIGAN CAREER CENTER, *[Month, Year – Present]*

- Coached 92 Career Center clients during their job transitions to identify steps necessary to land employment. Achieved 60% client job placement rate compared to the center average of 37%.

- Translated job training materials into Spanish. Created online tutorials -- increasing client usage by 33%.

- *"I've known Jill in the 18 months since she's joined the Career Center. She's is a top performer with a self-motivated, proactive "can do" attitude. She readily identifies opportunities to better serve our clients. She goes the extra mile and has made our Center function more effectively with her initiative. Unfortunately, federal funding for our Center has been cut. I love to retain her, if the budget allows. She is a terrific asset to any team."*
  --Gilbert G. Johnson, Senior Executive Vice President, State of Michigan Career Center

Events Coordinator, AMERICAN RED CROSS, *[Month, Year - Month, Year]*

- Ranked as #2 out of 27 recruiters for the Red Cross' "Celebrating America" special event.

- *"Jill excelled at recruiting volunteers and sponsors for this event. I worked with her personally as Executive Sponsor and found her to be savvy, persuasive and exceptional in her ability to communicate and influence people of diverse backgrounds – both business executives and individual contributors. I would gladly welcome the opportunity to work with her again."*
  --Hillary D. Wellington, Regional Vice-President & Interim COO, American Red Cross

Sales Representative, ABERCROMBE & FITCH *[Month, Year – Month, Year]*

- Trained and helped on-board 28 administrative and sales employees from diverse cultural backgrounds.

Interpreter/Instructor, U.S. EMBASSY SCHOOL, Barcelona, Spain, *[Month, Year – Month, Year]*

- As official translator, facilitated communications between Americans living in Barcelona and local government.
- Developed training curriculum on "survival" techniques for Americans living abroad, which was incorporated into teaching program at the U.S. Embassy School.

LANGUAGE PROFICIENCIES

Fluent in Spanish and French.
Taught English Conversation to Spanish businessmen, spouses and children, while living in Barcelona for two years.

Resume 5: *Employed in 3 Companies in 4 Years*

CANDACE COOPER

1234 N. Main Street #123• Atlanta, GA • 12345
(555) 555-5558 • candace.cooper@email.com

SUMMARY

PROACTIVE HUMAN RESOURCES GENERALIST that seeks out and champions breakthrough ideas and initiatives. Quickly analyzes complex workplace problems and finds actionable, pragmatic solutions. Able to take tough stands and resolve difficult business and people issues effectively. *Skilled in:* Talent Management, Work/Life Initiatives, Employee Relations, Organization Development and Leading Project Teams.

PROFESSIONAL EXPERIENCE

Imagemax, Inc – *Global leader in still imagery, video music and online media products.*

MANAGER – HUMAN RESOURCES   *[Year] - Present*
Providing human resources leadership and guidance for 400 managers and graphic designers in the Online Media Group. Reporting jointly to HR Senior Director and GM of Online Media.

- **Proactively created "Leadership Roundtables"** and identified 14 online programs to accelerate the orientation and development of new managers. Results: 95% utilization rate and positive feedback.

- **Selected by Corporate Global HR to lead a 5-person project team** to update the corporate policy on flexible work arrangements. Outcomes:
  --Provided 6 recommendations for action -- 100% endorsed by senior management.
  --Led the new policy execution in 3 pilot groups, with a 92% employee satisfaction rate.
  --Full policy execution projected to improve retention annually by 3 percentage points or $3.3 million

- **Collaborated with department leaders to implement a 15% rightsizing** within their groups, saving $2.6 million. Provided managerial coaching, employee transition counseling and survivor assistance which minimized disruption to the business.

- **Contributed to a 12% reduction in the number of monthly employee complaints filed** and a reduction of management time spent on such complaints – by driving 6 improvements in Online Media's utilization of the company-wide job posting process.

- **On last two 360 results, scored 94%+ positive** on the "quality, effectiveness and timeliness of HR support provided to clients" (detailed documentation provided upon request).

Previous Related Experience:
SUPERVISOR - PEOPLE SYSTEMS, Apple *[Year] – [Year]*
SENIOR HUMAN RESOURCES ANALYST, Amazon   *[Year] – [Year]*
HUMAN RESOURCES ANALYST, Amazon *[Year] – [Year]*

EDUCATION & CERTIFICATIONS

M.S. Organization Psychology, *Purdue University*
B.S. Human Resources, *Cornell University*
Certification, Leadership Architect Facilitator, Lominger Internal, Minneapolis, MN
Certification, Targeted Selection System, Development Dimensions International (DDI)

Resume 6: Using the CAR (Challenge, Action, Result) Approach

LAMONT FREDRICKS
807 East Elm Place • Chicago, IL 61216
(312) 758-8915 • lamontfredricks@gmail.com

SUMMARY

**#1 Human Resources Executive for Largest Divisions of Two Organizations.
12+ Years of Business & Management Consulting Experience.**

Trusted Business Partner In Guiding Organizations Through Rapid Growth
And Turnaround Business Scenarios – In Corporate Office, Sales & Manufacturing Settings.

PROFESSIONAL EXPERIENCE

MIDWEST FOODS COMPANY, Chicago, IL
Director – Human Resources & Organization Development [Year] to Present

Challenge: Recruited to lead HR for Midwest's $7.5 billion snack food supply chain organization facing inefficient operations, exceedingly high turnover and lack of business alignment across locations. Scope of role impacted 4100 employees, 11 manufacturing plants, 9 distribution centers, and 125 HQ employees.

Action: Partnered with the Supply Chain leadership team to develop and drive an aggressive People Strategy that elevated Midwest's supply chain to "employer of choice" status and supported improved productivity and streamlined infrastructure costs.

Results:
- **Helped implement large-scale organization change** which consolidated 6 North American supply chain organizations into one single organization -- generating $12.5 million in cost savings. Served as HR leader on the executive design team.

- **Championed execution of talent optimization strategy** which cut key position turnover by 30%, improved leadership bench strength by 20% and increased diversity in leadership roles by 25%.

- **Developed innovative incentive compensation programs** which supported the introduction of a new crucial new product resulting in $25 million in sales above plan.

- **Improved retention of key people by 32%** over prior year's total through customized individual development planning and mentoring for our 16 highest potential managers.

WIP SYSTEMS INTERNATIONAL, Waukegan, IL
Director - Human Resources [Year] to [Year]
Director – Organization Development [Year] to [Year]

Challenge: Provide HR leadership for the largest division of this rapidly growing microchip company supporting $600 million in sales, 1700 employees, 7 manufacturing sites, 9 sales forces and 85 HQ personnel in marketing, finance and administration.

Action: Upon promotion to head all HR, developed and executed a comprehensive organization development and labor relations agenda that supported the growth in business performance and elimination of non-performing businesses.

-continued-

Resume 6: Page Two

LAMONT FREDRICKS' RESUME
Page 2 • (312) 758-8915 • lamontfredricks@gmail.com

***Director - Human Resources**   [Year] to [Year]*
***Director – Organization Development**   [Year] to [Year]...continued*

Results:
- **Put in place aggressive employee performance and reward systems** that contributed to the division achieving of 117% and 123% of business plan - after having had three consecutive years of below plan financial performance.

- **Co-led the restructuring of Marketing & Sales for improved performance** saving $3.3 million. Led initiatives to simplify work, flatten the organization by 2 levels, and smoothly close 3 sales offices.

- **Business divestitures.** Developed the "talent transition plan" to support the divestiture of two businesses with sales totaling $100 million. Did HR due diligence, developed retention/exit packages and communication plan resulting in the smooth transition of the business to the new owners.

- **Directed the labor negotiation of 3 union contracts** within budget and without a work stoppage. Developed strategies which successfully defended against two union organizing attempts.

PERFORMAX WORLDWIDE, St. Louis, MO
Senior Consultant – Organization & Talent Development   *[Year] to [Year]*

Challenge: Provide comprehensive organization development consulting & training for this well-known $2 billion management consulting firm in the areas of: Leadership Development, Team Effectiveness, Organization Design, Six Sigma and Change Management. Led staff of 5 trainers and in-house consultants. .

Action: Collaborated with 12 corporate clients to build more productive workforces and grow skills of their leadership talent – generating $30 million in sales for Performax.

Results:
- **Served as lead implementation consultant for the "Six Sigma employee engagement" model** within six $2 billion+ manufacturing organizations – which on average lowered their manufacturing costs per unit by 3.5%.

- **Designed & conducted management development training programs** aimed at middle to senior managers. Programs included: Managing Performance and Leading Change. Trained 1450 management employees in five companies with program evaluations that averaged 9.1 on a 10 scale.

- **Redesigned training and skill development programs** saving $155,000 and increasing the training utilization rate from 55% to 86%.

EDUCATION & CERTIFICATIONS

M.S. in Human Resources Management, *University Of Illinois*
B.S. in Industrial Management, *Purdue University*

Certified Six Sigma Employee Engagement Consultant

Resume 7: Outstanding HR Experience, But No Degree

MARY E. BATES, PHR

444 West Carlson Drive • Greene, SC 29615
(444) 449.7474 • mbates11@gmail.com

SUMMARY

Accomplished HR Leader with 12 years of diverse business experience in the following areas:

- **Strategic Planning** – Worked directly with senior leaders in the development of the HR long-range plan aligned to the division's business strategy.
- **New Talent Acquisition** – Recruited and staffed hard-to-fill positions in engineering, marketing and hourly manufacturing. Able to quickly and creatively acquire needed talent and lead orientations for large numbers of new people.
- **Compensation & Performance Management** – Managed compensation plans for 1800 employees. Co-introduced a 360-feedback tool to supplement performance appraisals for executives.
- **Legal Compliance** –Wrote and enforced numerous policies and procedures to ensure compliance with corporate, union, federal and state requirements. Well-versed in diversity, EEOC and Affirmative Action plans.
- **Talent Retention & Development** – Coordinated the mentoring and coaching program for high potential talent which improved their retention. Known as a champion for employee development.

Executive Endorsements:

"Mary is an excellent business leader who leads human resources by example and exemplifies what HR can do to add value to the business.."
-CEO, North East Services Corp

"Mary engages easily, leads collaboratively and makes things happen."
-CEO, Hanover Products

BUSINESS EXPERIENCE

NORTH EAST SERVICES, Greene, SC
Director, Human Resources – XYZ Division (Year - Present)

Challenge: Promoted to oversee the HR function for a rapidly growing diverse services division with 3 subsidiaries and $500 million in sales. Collaborated with senior leadership team on short- and long-term strategic human resource plans designed to accelerate growth in consumer services.

Leadership Scope: Directed a team of 4 HR managers and 6 indirect reports. Dotted line oversight of 3 field managers. Ensured that all programs, policies and procedures were regulatory compliant. Served on performance management and diversity committees. Managed an annual department budget of $5.5M.

Key Contributions & Results:

- **Responded to company's rapid growth.** Developed and implemented policies and programs for functions that included employment, compensation, benefits, performance management, training and development, employee relations and affirmative action within 6 months. Hired and groomed HR staff.

- **Supported an increased workforce of 1800 employees,** equating to a 200% growth rate in personnel in only 12 months. Supported 1,250 more employees with zero increase in HR staff and minimal overtime. Saved in benefit costs and additional taxes by 22% by using shared services.

- **Avoided a potential EEOC compliance issue** by researching various college programs, identifying a school with a large minority population and hosting a job fair. Successfully doubled diversity results for compliance that enabled the company to increase contract award fees by 27%. Passed 3 Office of Federal Contract Compliance Programs (OFCCP) audits.

- **Stopped a union organizing** effort by working collaborating with legal counsel to plan activities in accord with National Labor Relations Board (NLRB). Saved the company annual labor rate hikes of up to 9% and protected company's reputation with an important client.

continued....

Resume 7: Page Two

MARY E. BATES, PHR

Page 2 • (444) 449.7474 • mbates11@gmail.com

NORTH EAST SERVICES, *continued...*
Manager, Human Resources – ABC Division (Year - Year)

Recruited for this position by former manager. Developed, staffed and directed human resources department for an organization with 400+ employees. Led staff of 10.

Key Contributions & Results:

- **Within first two weeks of hire, assessed HR department of a new acquisition** and made recommendations to executive management on departmental requirements.

- **Built an HR department from scratch**, and trained a new staff comprised of a benefits manager, 4 recruiters, 2 generalists and a clerk – all within the first 18 months.

- **Facilitated the company's hire of 205 employees across 29 states** and a 3-week transition for an EPSSA contract, the largest in company's history. Traveled to each site to meet with management, make presentations, and provide benefits briefings.

BOEING GROUP, Chicago, IL
Area Manager – Human Resources (Year – Year)

Managed staffing, performance management and employee relations for 127 aerospace employees. Headed up employee engagement, safety & health and site communications committees. Led office staff of 5.

Key Contributions & Results:

- **Improved the organization and maintenance of safety & health activities by 100%,** ensuring compliance with Department of Labor and Illinois state regulations.

- **Reduced on site security violations by 60%** by implementing rigorous protocols and procedures.

- **Contributed to a 30% improvement in employee engagement results,** in close collaboration with the leadership team, through aggressive organization surveying and targeted follow-up actions.

GATORADE COMPANY, Atlanta, GA
Plant Office Manager (Year – Year)

- Set up all administrative procedures and human resources functions for a 300-person manufacturing plant.

Previous Related Experience: (Year -Year)
Worked as an Executive Assistant in positions of increasing responsibility. Gained experience in interviewing, hiring, training and supervising staff. Supported budgeting, HRIS and financial reporting. Obtained skills in management services, contract negotiations and management, and drafting proposals.

PROFESSIONAL DEVELOPMENT & AFFILIATIONS

PHR certified (Year)
New Hampshire College – six classes short of attaining B.S. in Human Resources.
Completed Six Sigma black belt certification

Society for Human Resource Management (SHRM)
American Society for Training & Development (ASTD)
The Human Resource Planning Society (HRPS)

Resume 8: HR Professional With Line Management Experience

OLIVIA McFEE

888-888-8888 • omcfee2377@yahoo.com
2336 Pennsylvania Drive • Brandon, FL 337021

SUMMARY

HR LEADER – WITH GENERAL MANAGEMENT AND P&L EXPERIENCE.
Skilled at rapidly attracting, developing and optimizing talent. Operated a $100 million business with full P&L accountability. Served as the "go-to" HR leader for senior operating executives on multiple acquisitions -- from due diligence to conversion. Documented HR results in the following areas:

- Performance Management
- Employee Relations
- HR Information Systems (HRIS)
- Employee Engagement
- Mergers & Acquisitions
- Organization Development
- Compensation
- Recruitment
- Labor Relations

EXPERIENCE

HARRIS RESTAURANT GROUP, *#2 restaurant chain in North America.*
Promoted rapidly through a series of increasingly responsible divisional HR leadership roles in the U.S. Provided HR guidance to senior leadership teams during store acquisitions and new restaurant openings for North America.

ASST. GENERAL MANAGER - OPERATIONS & HUMAN RESOURCES *[Year]-[Year]*
SOUTHEAST U.S. RESTAURANT DIVISION, Brandon, Florida

> **Delivered record profitability of $14 million for these 12 restaurants with 550 employees and staff. Functioned as the "Operations-second-in-command" to the GM – while leading the Human Resources function as well. Won the President's "Eagle Award for Excellence."**

- Increased revenue by 21% year-on-year and improved restaurant seating rate from 75% to 91%.
- Improved customer satisfaction to an avg. of 98.7% & earned record results in cost of food sold.
- Co-developed a new "Get It Here!" department to upsell new customers, enhance customer experience and meet and maintain Harris' standards.
- Designed and led a grand three-day "Welcome to Harris" event for 200 associates following restaurant acquisition.
- Improved employee engagement results from 55% to 83% total engagement – best in the organization.

DIRECTOR of HUMAN RESOURCES *[Year]-[Year]*
WEST COAST U.S. RESTAURANT DIVISION, Phoenix, Arizona

> **HR executive for 10 restaurants challenged with retaining workforce during and after two union organizing drives. Successfully retained 97% of key talent while spearheading two triumphant union avoidance campaigns and avoiding $2.6M in potential overhead cost increases.**

- Following the de-unionization efforts, introduced six new employee programs that helped stabilize the business and improved employee engagement survey results by 21 percent points.
- Partnered with the local government to create a first-ever "Phoenix After Dark" program which honored employees and their families at the property -- which also dramatically improved morale & retention.

- continued-

Resume 8: Page Two

OLIVA McFEE – Page Two   888-888-8888 • omcfee2377@yahoo.com

DIRECTOR of HUMAN RESOURCES   [Year]-[Year]
MIDWEST U.S. RESTAURANT DIVISION, Chicago, Illinois
Served as head of HR supporting six restaurants employing 225 employees. Reported to the General
Manager of the Midwest Division.

> **Championed innovative plan which increased employee utilization from 72% to 86% during
> non-peak operating periods. Plan included short-term rotating layoffs, short work weeks
> and other strategies. Personally selected by CEO to share these best practices with four
> other sites.**

- Improved employee survey results by 11 percentage-points through enhanced communications, store
  manager engagement and innovative employee recognition programs.
- Decreased employee hiring, recruitment and staffing costs 7% annually.
- Reduced number of employee accidents by 5% and days out of work through improved training and
  incentive programs that encouraged employees to work safer and smarter.

MOTOROLA, *Global leader in wireless communications*
MANAGER of HUMAN RESOURCES   [Year]-[Year]
Corporate Headquarters, Chicago, Illinois

- Spearheaded the headquarters diversity and inclusion initiative. Improved representation of women and
  people of color in hard-to-fill positions by 11% and 14% respectively.
- Launched a "One Company" college recruitment program which consolidated our campus recruitment
  efforts across Motorola locations which cut our staffing costs by $185,000.

BLUE CROSS BLUE SHIELD, *Largest health insurer in North America.*
SUPERVISOR, COMPENSATION & BENEFITS   [Year]-[Year]
Regional Sales Division, Munster, Indiana
**Launched career as Compensation Specialist in [Year], promoted to Compensation Supervisor in [Year]
and promoted to Supervisor of Compensation & Benefits in [Year] to [Year].**

- In collaboration with the corporate group, led the development of new base pay and incentive compensation programs for 325 sales and marketing associates linked to corporate
  revenues.

EDUCATION

UNIVERSITY OF MICHIGAN, Advanced HR Executive Program
UNIVERSITY OF CINCINATTI, Bachelor of Science (B.S.)

PROFESSIONAL AFFILIATIONS

Senior HR Practitioner, The Human Resources Planning Society.
Society for Human Resource Management (SHRM), Program Committee

Resume 9: *Customizing Resume For A Specific HR Job*

MORGAN S. JOHNSON, PHR
10099 Carter Circle • Cleveland, OH 34788
mjjohnson@sbcglobal.net • (454) 467-9044

CANDIDATE FOR HR DIRECTOR – AT CHEVRON OIL

SUMMARY OF QUALIFICATIONS: Human Resources Executive with 11 years of proven experience working with senior management on Talent Management strategies which drive business results in oil and energy companies. Certified HR professional with broad knowledge of approaches to optimize talent in a variety of workplaces including corporate, sales, union and non-union environments. Proven track record and superior abilities in the following areas:

♦ Talent Management	♦ Training & Development	♦ Employee Relations
♦ Employee Retention	♦ Compensation & Benefits	♦ Change Management

PROFESSIONAL EXPERIENCE

Brown Energy Corporation, Cleveland, OH   *[Year] - Present*
HUMAN RESOURCES DIRECTOR. Reported to Vice Chairman of this 10-year old commercial gas, fuel and oil company. Transformed HR from administrative role to strategic talent management function.

Key Contributions:

♦ **Worked with the senior leadership team** to put in place a new performance and reward program that contributed to the achievement of 127% of business plan on average for last three years.

♦ **Rebuilt employee benefits program** by consolidating providers and renegotiating contracts. Successfully maintained benefit costs with 1% increase in premium over 3 years and achieved savings of $120,000 in first year.

♦ **Established retention strategies which cut turnover** in key positions in Marketing, Sales and Manufacturing to 1.5%.

♦ **Helped re-position the company as an "employer of choice"** in the local area for engineering and hourly talent, resulting in virtual elimination of all external search costs.

Allied Home Construction Corporation, Cleveland, OH   *[Year] – [Year]*
SENIOR HUMAN RESOURCES MANAGER. Reported to the VP - Human Resourcesfor this nationwide home builder with $570 Million in annual revenues and 1200 exempt and non-exempt employees over 27 locations. Managed an HR staff of 5. Key contributor in driving leading edge variable compensation plan used as an effective recruiting tool. Collaborated with the technology group to design a comprehensive applicant tracking system to integrate with current HRIS. Linked HR initiatives to the Allied's strategic business plan.

Key Contributions:

♦ **Served as sole non-VP employee selected to Executive Leadership Council.** Provided ongoing tactical support and advice in setting growth objectives for the corporation.

♦ **Conducted extensive recruiting as sole recruiter** accountable for filling 126 management, technical and professional positions in 3 years. 92% client satisfaction rate with quality of hires.

♦ **Introduced brand new on-boarding program** and employee training, resulting in a 94% satisfaction score.

♦ **Co-developed a new succession planning initiative** which lowered hiring costs by 25% over 3 years.

♦ **Led four successful union avoidance campaigns** covering 700 employees.

♦ **Reduced the "time-to-fill" rate** for all job vacancies from 65 days to 32 days using innovative staffing strategies.

-continued-

Resume 9: Page Two

MORGAN S. JOHNSON, PHR   Page 2 • (454) 467-9044 • jjohnson@sbcglobal.net

Holiday Real Estate Corporation, Lexington, KY   [Year] – [Year]
DIRECTOR OF HUMAN RESOURCES. Led the first-ever Human Resources function for this $225 Million business subsidiary of Century 21 with over 600 employees in 11 locations. Managed staff of 5. Worked with management to create a performance management system, progressive discipline policy and recruitment policy guidelines for hourly and salaried employees. Led the implementation of the flexible benefits plan, incentive pay and compensation programs.

Key Contributions:
- **Launched talent acquisition function**, reducing staffing expenses by $275,000.
- **Worked with senior leadership to flatten organization by two levels**, close two sales offices and rationalize administrative staff by 25%.
- **Led the successful negotiation of two union contracts** within budgeted costs and without a work stoppage.

Exxon Mobil, Irving, TX   [Year] – [Year]
World's largest oil refiner with 80,000 employees. Rapidly promoted from an entry-level HR Representative role to Supervisor – Human Resources Development then to Manager -- Talent Acquisition.

MANAGER – TALENT ACQUISITION. During a period of significant growth, accountable for recruiting and staffing all marketing and sales positions for the Southwest division (the largest division of the company). Led staff of two. Spearheaded the national college recruitment program, special executive searches and targeted acquisition of talent up through the Senior Director levels of the corporation.

Key Contributions:
- Met cost per hire objectives & aggressive hiring goals of 110-120 hires/ year for 2 straight years.
- Attained 95% satisfaction score from hiring managers on the recruitment process and results -- as measured by the corporate annual survey.
- Attained 92% satisfaction score from candidates hired six months after their employment – best score in the Company!

SUPERVISOR – HUMAN RESOURCES DEVELOPMENT. As part of an elite Exxon Mobil corporate task force, provided company-wide training for supervisors and middle managers on "Managing People & Performance."
- Trained 850 management employees. Training program evaluations averaged 9.2 on a 10 scale.

HUMAN RESOURCES REPRESENTATIVE. Entry-level HR role supporting the Employee Relations and Compensation & Benefits groups.
- Participated in a designing innovative incentive pay program for 450 unionized employees.

EDUCATION & PROFESSIONAL AFFILIATIONS

INDIANA STATE UNIVERSITY, Terre Haute, IN
Bachelor of Arts Degree, Sociology

Certified Professional in Human Resources (PHR)
Society for Human Resources Management (SHRM)
American Society for Training & Development (ASTD)

Resume 10: Recognized For HR Excellence

MARGARET DOREN

1122 Shoney Drive, Cranbury, NJ 08512
609-555-2345, margdoren@yahoo.com

SUMMARY

Human Resources Executive – Recognized For Excellence.
- Trusted advisor to senior leadership on talent management and transformational change.
- Pro at reorganizing and integrating businesses for aggressive growth.
- Reputation for flawless execution of key HR priorities & initiatives.

EXPERIENCE

GLOBAL COSMETICS, Cranbury, NJ

Executive Director, Human Resources & Talent Development (Year to Present)

Recruited to lead the HR function for an $800 million, 2100 person turnaround global women's cosmetics business. Managed a team of 12 HR professionals. Accountable for strategic HR planning, talent management, building organizational and employee capabilities, facilitating transformational change, and building effective working relationships with employees, unions, customers, and suppliers to increase revenues and profit by 30% per year. Reporting directly to the CEO.

- **Won Chairman's Award For HR Excellence for last two years** for leadership in driving the major business consolidation of several divisions into one market-focused organization. This initiative helped improve operating profit by $25M
- **Developed and implemented a new performance management process** focused on building employee capabilities that aligned with the organization's new 18% growth objective.
- **Hired 15 senior executives into key leadership roles** and by leading one-on-one executive coaching and executive team-level interventions.
- **Supported aggressive growth plan** by recruiting 300 employees for 2 field operations in 6 months

FEDERAL RESTAURANT CORPORATION, Newark, NJ

Human Resource Manager – Corporate Headquarters (Year to Year)

Key HR contributor for a $1.5 Billion organization with 12,800 employees across North America. Responsible for developing, implementing, and aligning human resources and payroll functions of a startup business with corporate objectives. Reported directly to the VP, Human Resources.

- **Developed a new employee incentive plan** that delivered 30% higher customer service measures than the company average.
- **Streamlined an outdated operation to function with 12% fewer employees** by creating and implementing a training strategy which increased employee flexibility and productivity.
- **Reduced OFCCP/EEOC charges** and employee grievances by 80% over prior year.

-continued-

Resume 10: Page Two

MARGARET DOREN
Page 2 - 609-555-2345 - margdoren@yahoo.com

FEDERAL RESTAURANT CORPORATION, *(continued)*

Human Resource Manager – Eastern Region   *(Year to Year)*

Supported an employee population of 4,500. Managed all aspects of talent acquisition, employee development, compensation, policy administration, and employee relations. Directly supervised a staff of 4 HR professionals.

- **Supported a 225% expansion of business operations** across North America through increased management succession capability through internal development and external recruiting.
- **Created an innovative staffing, onboarding and training process** that reduced cost per hire by 50% and contributed to improved restaurant profitability by 3.5%.

AMERICAN OIL CORPORATION, Dallas, TX

Sales Territory Manager,   *(Year to Year)*

Developmental assignment in sales operations with overall P&L responsibility for 35 gas retail operations, both company-owned and franchise-operated.

Human Resource Generalist   *(Year to Year)*

Responsible for staffing, compensation administration, and counseling on management development issues. Conduct various organizational effectiveness initiatives. Manage employee relations issues, and HR policies and practices for 500 employees.

- **Helped implement a major organizational development initiative** to establish a new division of engineering consultants in a large refinery in Texas.

QUAKER OATS COMPANY, Chicago, IL

Compensation Analyst   *(Year to Year)*

Responsible for administration and analysis of the salaried compensation program. Conducted 52 salary surveys for positions up to the Director-level utilizing the Hay Process and internal pay benchmarking.

EDUCATION & AWARDS

Hofstra University, Long Island, NY
Master of Arts, Organizational Psychology 3.9/4.0 GPA

Northwestern University, Evanston, IL
Bachelor of Science, Psychology, 3.7/4.0 GPA

Voted One of the "Top 50 HR Directors of the Year" by *HR Magazine* [Year]

Resume 11: Targeting a Specific Geographic Area (California)

STEVEN BUCKNER, PHR-CA

14 Manheim Drive ♦ San Jose, CA 90000 ♦ (764) 555-5555 ♦ sbuckner67@yahoo.com

SUMMARY

**Certified Professional in Human Resources (PHR) and state certified in California (PHR-CA).
Extensive experience as an HR generalist in attracting, developing and retaining talent.**
Expert in HR-regulations and legal mandates specific to the state of California. Proven success in
building teams, negotiating win-win agreements and developing employee policies.

EXPERIENCE

BLUE KNIGHT CORPORATION – San Jose, CA
*$3 billion+ organization providing voice, touch and online communications systems for mid-sized
companies.*

HUMAN RESOURCES MANAGER, *[YEAR] to Present*
Recruited specifically for HR experience in California to help open new 300-employee, $400 million
customer service center in San Jose. Guided the staffing, startup and management of a full spectrum
of HR operations, systems and programs in record time. Worked with executive leadership team to
create HR practices needed to attract, orient and compensate key talent.

- **Played a key role in ensuring the successful launch of San Jose service center.** Personal
  efforts were cited as the driving force behind branch's employee-retention rate of 89% within an
  industry where less than 75% is the norm.

- **Negotiated approximately 50 salary offers** and dozens of sign-on bonuses/relocation packages
  annually at both the exempt and nonexempt level.

- **Brought workers' compensation program into 100% full compliance.** Instituted preferred
  providers list and trained managers and associates on procedures to follow in case of injury.

- **Reduced benefits costs by 15%** annually through meticulous recordkeeping and ensuring that
  company did not pay for benefits for which employees were ineligible.

- **Introduced company's first formal performance review program at the service center,**
  creating a flexible and well - received tool that was later adopted company-wide.

- **Revised job descriptions across all levels and 25+ categories.** "Shadowed" and interviewed
  employees to construct an accurate picture of the duties and skills required for each position.

FRITO LAY – Fairfax, CA
#2 manufacturing location of world's largest snacks and chips manufacturer.

PLANT HUMAN RESOURCES SUPERVISOR, *[YEAR] to [YEAR]*
HUMAN RESOURCES REPRESENTATIVE, *[YEAR] to [YEAR]*
Promoted in six months from Rep to Supervisor to provide HR support for a non-union employee
population of 550. Managed recruitment, training, benefits, and employee relations. Co-chaired
annual flex-enrollment meetings, resolved conflicts between employees and insurance carriers,
coordinated health fairs to promote employee wellness and performed exit interviews.

-continued-

Resume 11: Page Two

STEVEN BUCKNER, PHR-CA
Page 2 ♦ (764) 555-5555 ♦ sbuckner67@yahoo.com

HUMAN RESOURCES SUPERVISOR, *[YEAR] to [YEAR]*
HUMAN RESOURCES REPRESENTATIVE, *[YEAR] to [YEAR]... continued*

- **Trained 25-member management team** on interviewing techniques and best practices. Conducted workshops and one-on-one coaching sessions that improved our candidate offer/acceptance ratio by 18%.

- **Saved company $15,000/month** on average by reducing reliance on employment agencies. In-sourced previously outsourced talent acquisition functions and reduced billable hours from 200+ to less than 15 per month.

- **Co-developed company's first-ever standardized disciplinary procedures** and tracking system that insulated company from legal risk and ensured consistent and fair discipline processes.

- **Contributed to an improvement in the plant's employee engagement survey results by 12%** by devising innovative pay-for –performance and morale-boosting programs.

EDUCATION & CERTIFICATIONS

B.A. in Psychology (with honors) -- Michigan State University
PHR-CA -- Certified Professional in Human Resources in California
PHR – Certified Professional in Human Resources

PROFESSIONAL DEVELOPMENT

Completing ongoing training in the areas of compensation and benefits, employee and labor relations, leaves of absence, workers' compensation and workplace safety/security – **all specific to the state of California.**

AFFILIATIONS

Society for Human Resource Management (SHRM)
Staffing Management Association (SMA) of Southern CA

Resume 12: BEFORE Version - Functional Resume

Thea Jones

2347 Delaware Road, North Kingstown, RI 06020
(401) 345-9987, TheaJones@lakeview.com

Summary

HR PROFESSIONAL -- With Eleven Years of Proven Leadership & Consulting Experience delivering comprehensive, integrated HR and talent management solutions. Created and transformed non-existent or under-performing HR departments into value-added, strategic organizational partners. Both private and public sector experience in HR with organizations ranging from 500-7000 employees. Skilled in:

• Talent Management	• Employee/Labor Relations	• Diversity & Inclusion
• Compensation	• Labor/Chief Spokesman	• Safety
• Performance Management	• Culture Change	• Recruitment /Staffing
• Employee Benefits	• Compliance	• HRIS

Professional Experience

TALENT MANAGEMENT (11 YEARS)

- Planned and implemented HR functions for two plant startups in Dallas and San Antonio, TX (220 & 300 FTEs, respectively).
- Reduced turnover at a foods plant from 37% to 18% over a one year period utilizing a variety of interventions.
- Implemented three reductions-in-force using early separation, attrition, schedule changes, and facility closures eliminating 1200 positions saving $100M over a four year period, balancing cash flow availability to minimize reductions.
- Developed position control system which eliminated overstaffing, improved forecasting, federal reporting, and master scheduling of staff. Saved $1.2M per year from zero-based hiring.
- Improved minority retention from 67% to 88% through improved relationships with HBCUs, faith-based organizations and community groups through the establishment of a "Grow Our Own" program.
- Implemented profile tools to predict teacher success and improve retention, expanded mentoring program through grants resulting in improved performance and retention, implemented improvements in background investigation and record-keeping.
- Successfully managed audits/complaints with EEOC, OFCCP, DOL, SPBR, SERB, Civil Service, civil courts.

LABOR/EMPLOYEE RELATIONS (8 YEARS)

- Managed both union and non-union locations. Experience with 8 international unions in both private/public sectors. Grievance administration through arbitration advocacy, mediation, ADR.
- Chief spokesperson in concurrent negotiations with largest teacher's union in Ohio. Achieved inflationary caps on healthcare, multi-tier wage schedules, consolidated multiple schedules and improved work rules, etc. No work stoppages.
- Led a culture change initiative that resulted in decertification of a 350 employee local, led by the union's vice president.

COMPENSATION/BENEFITS; (10 YRS)

- Designed and implemented various skill-based, performance-based, traditional and executive compensation programs.
- Identified/problem-solved a $21M underfunding situation without impacting current budget, preventing greater cuts.
- Implemented value-based health plans, wellness programs, eligibility audits, facilitated labor/management committees.
- Identified illegal practice between broker and carrier resulting in awards to the employer, license suspensions for offenders, and changes in state legislation regarding transparency and broker compensation.
- Successfully managed two FLSA audits.

-continued...

Resume 12: BEFORE Version - Page Two

Thea Jones
Page 2 - (401) 345-9987 - TheaJones@lakeview.com

PERFORMANCE MANAGEMENT & TRAINING; (8 YRS)
- Redesigned administrative and classified performance evaluation tools implementing objective metrics.
- Designed/implemented literacy, skilled-trade apprenticeship, machine operator, safety, & quality training programs
- Delivered supervisor and leadership training. (Certified Interaction Management Trainer, DDI)
- Designed and implemented E-Onboarding including training for harassment, discrimination, safety, orientation.
- Project Lead/Lead Trainer for Continuous Improvement and ISO implementations (Mfg).

HRIS/TECHNOLOGY; (5 YRS)
- Project lead on 7 HRIS implementations using multiple platforms, software solutions, industries; two included integrated payroll systems, and two included automated time & attendance.
- Project lead on a $1M platform upgrade from a simple peer-to-peer network to a WAN with server farm using VoIP.

SAFETY & PAYROLL; (5 YRS).
- Supervised non-HR functions of Purchasing, Technology, Payroll
- Served as Director of Operations for a third party benefits administrator providing services to self-funded groups ranging from 200-3500 FTE, responsible for claims payment, plan building, eligibility, customer service, FSA/HSA/HRA, stop loss, consultation, etc. for self-funded clients. Assumed "backroom" services for a 100K life carrier under investigation with Dept. of Insurance. Resurrected carrier business without losing any prior clients.

Employment History

HUMAN RESOURCES CONSULTANT – North Kingston, RI, [YEAR] - Present

EASTERN ILLINOIS UNIVERSITY – Charleston, IL
Director of Human Resources, [YEAR] - [YEAR]

CLEVELAND SCHOOL DISTRICT – Cleveland, OH
Director of Human Resources, [YEAR] - [YEAR]

GARY CITY SCHOOLS – Gary, IN
Director of Human Resources, [YEAR] - [YEAR]

RICHMOND CITY SCHOOLS – Richmond, IN
Director of Administrative Services, [YEAR] - [YEAR]

UNIVERSAL BENEFITS CORP – Richmond, IN
Director of Operations, [YEAR] - [YEAR]

QUAKER OATS COMPANY – Danville, IL
Employee Relations Manager, [YEAR] - [YEAR]

DEAN FOODS – Dallas, TX and San Antonio, TX
Employee Relations Manager, [YEAR] - [YEAR]
Training Supervisor, [YEAR] - [YEAR]
HR Trainee, [YEAR] - [YEAR]

Education

M.B.A. Eastern Illinois University, (4.0 GPA)
B.B.A. (Human Resources), Wayne State University (3.75 GPA)

Resume 12: AFTER Version – Reverse Chronological Resume

THEA JONES

2347 Delaware Road • North Kingstown, RI 06020
(401) 345-9987 • TheaJones@kingston.com

Summary

HUMAN RESOURCES PROFESSIONAL --- With Eleven Years of Proven Leadership & Consulting Experience helping organizations deliver better results through the optimum utilization of their talent. Created and transformed under-performing HR departments into value-added organizational partners. Both private and public sector experience with organizations ranging from 500-7000 employees. Skilled in:

• Employee/Labor Relations	• Talent Management	• Diversity & Inclusion
• Labor/Chief Spokesman	• Compensation	• Safety
• Culture Change	• Performance Management	• Recruitment /Staffing
• Compliance	• Employee Benefits	• HRIS

Experience

MANAGING DIRECTOR & OWNER [Year – Present]
Kingston Human Capital Consulting, LLC – North Kingstown, RI,
Independent consulting firm established to provide human capital advisory and consulting services in limited engagements.

- Retained by rapidly-growing $25 million printing company to successfully manage audits/complaints with EEOC, OFCCP, DOL, SPBR, SERB, Civil Service, civil courts.
- In process of developing comprehensive human capital strategy for a large, local non-profit association designed to improve member retention by 30% and leadership development for 25 key executives.

DIRECTOR – HUMAN RESOURCES [Year – Year]
Eastern Illinois University – Charleston, IL
Cleveland School District – Cleveland, OH
Gary City Schools – Gary, IN

- **Chief spokesperson in negotiations with largest teacher's union in Ohio.** Achieved inflationary caps on healthcare, multi-tier wage schedules, consolidated multiple schedules and improved work rules – with a work stoppage.
- **Implemented three reductions-in-force** using early separation, schedule changes and facility closures eliminating 1200 positions saving $60M over a three year period.
- **Implemented profile tools to predict teacher success and improve retention,** expanded mentoring program through grants resulting in improved performance and retention, implemented improvements in background investigation and record-keeping.
- **Successfully managed audits/complaints** with EEOC, OFCCP, DOL, SPBR, SERB, Civil Service, civil courts.
- **Identified/problem-solved a $21M underfunding situation** without impacting current budget, preventing greater cuts.
- **Implemented value-based health plans,** wellness programs, eligibility audits, facilitated labor/management committees.
- **Identified illegal practice between a broker and carrier** resulting in awards to the employer, license suspensions for offenders, and changes in state legislation regarding transparency and broker compensation.
- **Designed and implemented various key compensation programs** -- skill-based programs, performance-based compensation, traditional and executive compensation programs.

-continued-

Resume 12: AFTER Version - Page 2

THEA JONES
Page 2 • (401) 345-9987 • TheaJones@kingston.com

DIRECTOR OF OPERATIONS [Year – Year]
Universal Benefits Corp – Richmond, IN

- **Led Operations for this third party benefits administrator** providing services to self-funded groups ranging from 200-3500 FTE, responsible for claims payment, plan building, eligibility, customer service, FSA/HSA, stop loss, consultation, etc. for self-funded clients.
- **Project lead on 7 HRIS implementations** using multiple platforms, software solutions, industries; two included integrated payroll systems, and two included automated time & attendance.
- **Project lead on $1 million platform upgrade** from a simple peer-to-peer network to a WAN with server farm using VoIP.

EMPLOYEE RELATIONS MANAGER – QUAKER OATS [Year – Year]
Second largest food manufacturing plant in Danville, IL

- **Reduced turnover from 37% to 18%** over a one year period utilizing a variety of interventions.
- **Developed innovative position control system** which eliminated overstaffing, improved forecasting, federal reporting, and master scheduling of staff. Saved $1.2M per year from zero-based hiring.
- **Led a culture change initiative** that resulted in decertification of a 350 employee local, led by the union's vice president.
- **Improved minority retention from 67% to 88%** through improved relationships with HBCUs, faith-based organizations and community groups through the establishment of a "Grow Our Own" program.

HUMAN RESOURCES GENERALIST -- DEAN FOODS [Year – Year]
Employee Relations Manager – Dallas, TX
Training Supervisor – San Antonio, TX
HR Trainee – San Antonio, TX

- **Promoted through a variety of positions** in the process of planning and implementing HR functions for two plant startups in Dallas and San Antonio, TX (220 and 300 FTE, respectively).
- **Designed/implemented training programs** for literacy, skilled-trade apprenticeship, machine operator, safety, & quality.
- **Delivered supervisor and leadership training.** (Certified Interaction Management Trainer, DDI)
- **Project Lead/Lead Trainer** for Continuous Improvement and ISO implementations (Mfg).

Education

M.B.A. Eastern Illinois University, (4.0 GPA)
B.B.A. (Human Resources), Wayne State University (3.75 GPA)

Resume 13: Universal Resume Highlighting Important Keywords

TOM BLAKELY, PH.D.
234 Elm Street • Mayberry, NC 21640
(309) 758-8111 • tom_blakely@email.com

SUMMARY

TALENT & ORGANIZATION DEVELOPMENT LEADER with seven years experience partnering with business executives in driving improved organization and employee performance. PhD and professionally certified in various assessment tools used to build leadership capability. Exceptional skills in:

➢ Talent Management	➢ Leadership Development	➢ Organization Surveys
➢ 360 Degree Feedback	➢ Mergers & Acquisitions	➢ Change Management
➢ Organization Development	➢ Performance Management	➢ Succession Planning

EXPERIENCE

NATIONAL AIRLINES -- *Third largest global airline with 30,000 employees and revenues of $28 billion.*

Senior Manager - Talent & Organization Development [Year] – [Year]
Promoted to drive the talent and organization development agenda for staff located at corporate HQ. Collaborated with key HQ leaders on succession planning, high potential development, employee surveys, 360-degree feedback and performance management.

- **Led the talent review and succession planning process** for the Marketing and R&D groups. Results were used to improve the bench strength of these groups by 25% and 12% respectively.
- **Co-developed the first web-based curriculum** of in-house leadership development courses - saving $280,000 in travel costs and consultant fees. Course utilization has improved by 25% and client feedback averages 9.1/10 scale.
- **Co-developed and implemented an innovative "sales success predictor tool"** for all new sales hires resulting in an 11% reduction in sales attrition over the previous year.
- **Aggressively project managed the employee engagement survey process** for 400 customer service employees. Outcomes: 60+ improvement plans were developed…85% of plans were completed within 9 months…12% rise in engagement results occurred within 12 months.
- **As a key leader on the Business Development Due Diligence Team** identified key talent issues for a $300 million new acquisition which will add 10% to company revenues.
- **Appointed by CEO to provide coaching** to 12 senior VPs on their 360 feedback development plans.

Manager - Training & Development [Year] – [Year]
Hired as lead trainer and to provide oversight for in-house trainers and external providers of training services.   Managed annual budget of $20 million for tuition reimbursement and professional certification programs.

- **Collaborated with HR Directors to design and co-lead training for 225 managers** on "Effectively Coaching & Developing Employees." Program feedback averaged 9.2/10 and drove a visible improvement in the "quality of coaching" score on organization survey results
- **Co-trained over 150 new Customer Service Managers and 2,300 new employees** on performance management to support the corporation's 20% increase in over-the-phone customer service support.

-continued-

Resume 13: Page Two

TOM BLAKELY, PH.D.
Page 2 • tom_blakely@email.com • (309) 758-8111

WALGREENS -- Largest *drug retailing chain in the US with 8000 stores with $70 billion in revenue.*

Human Resources Generalist, Eastern Sector   [Year] – [Year]
Chief HR point of contact for stores in New York, New Jersey and Virginia on employee relations, performance management and compensation issues.

- Managed the store staffing position control system for 120 stores in the Eastern Sector which eliminated overstaffing, improved physical working conditions and the skills of supervisors.
- Oversaw and implemented the merit pay system based on performance evaluations designed to reward top performing 10%.
- Wrote new Employee Policy & Procedures Manuals detailing comprehensive guidelines covering 1500 management and pharmacy employees which reduced training time and improved consistency.

Analyst, Employee Performance & Development, Corporate Headquarters   [Year] – [Year]
Hired as intern and promoted in three months to Analyst to strengthen project support in the EP&D group.

- Creatively developed the first-ever performance management guide and tool kit still in use for 2000 Drug Store Managers.
- Helped redesign performance evaluation tool and trained 200 nonexempt and administrative employees on effective utilization.

EDUCATION

Ph.D. Organization Psychology, *Columbia University*
M.S. in Organization Development, *Georgia State University*
B.S. in Biology, *Purdue University*

CERTIFICATIONS

HOGAN Development Assessments
Lominger Tools (VOICES 360, Learning Agility)
Myers-Briggs Type Indicator (MBTI)

Korn/Ferry Leadership Styles
Strengths Finder
Profilor 360 Degree Feedback

Resume 14: Accentuating Board & Comp Committee Experience

Clare S. Rodriguez

403 Echo Circle, Detroit, MI 423465 • 602.211.1999 • clare-rod12@email.com

SUMMARY

EXPERIENCED CHIEF COMPENSATION & BENEFITS EXECUTIVE. Proven track record in designing, developing and executing executive, employee and sales compensation programs which drive productivity. Certified Compensation Professional (CCP) that excels in deadline-driven, rapidly changing environments. Experience working with Boards of Directors and Compensation Committees. Team builder, meticulous problem solver with strong influencing skills.

BUSINESS EXPERIENCE

GENERAL SYSTEMS CORPORATION – Detroit, MI
$2 billion computer hardware services company headquartered in Detroit with 25 locations across the U.S. and Canada.

Vice President, Compensation & Benefits *(Year – Present)*

Head of the company's compensation & benefits function covering 15,000 employees reporting to SVP of HR. Chief point of contact for all employee benefit and compensation plans including: Cash & Equity Compensation, Benefit Programs and Perquisites. Health Care, Defined Benefit, Bonus, Sales Incentive and Deferred Compensation plans. Directed external consultants and managed third party benefit providers. Managed staff of 11.

Key Contributions:

- **Worked with top management and the Board of Directors** to create a new Total Rewards program that provided stronger link to performance and helped drive 12% average annual revenue growth for the last three years.

- **Designed a new equity incentive plan** for 375 North American executives that allowed increased individual choice. Program scored a 92% satisfaction rate among the executive population and contributed to an improvement in executive retention by 21%.

- **Reviewed new pension designs for compliance** with the company philosophy and ERISA legal guidelines. In Canada, moved from defined benefit to defined contribution, working with the HR group & work councils to gain approval. Projected savings: $32 million.

- **Executed 24 Health Care program improvements** which consolidated multiple HMOs into one national offering saving over $10 million with no decrease in employee satisfaction.

RANDGOLD FOOD COMPANY - Charlotte, North Carolina
$4 billion leader in food management and hospitality with 17,000 employees in locations throughout the US, Latin America and Canada.

Director – Compensation & Total Rewards (Year – Year)
Led the compensation function for the $2 billion Frozen Foods business unit with a client base of 7,200. Oversaw the HRIS and Health & Welfare function for entire organization. Key compensation advisor to the Frozen Foods Division President and her senior leadership team. .

Key Contributions:

- **Established new performance-based salary structure and grading system** in collaboration with the Frozen Foods senior leadership team. Effort also consolidated redundant positions reducing headcount by 9% and eliminating $2 million in non-value added work.

- **Implemented PeopleSoft within one fiscal year for all 17,000 employees** in the U.S., Latin America and Canada. Implementation was near-flawless, streamlined HR processes and provided $17 million savings in HR-related expenses.

--continued--

Resume 14: Page Two

Clare S. Rodriguez – Page 2
602.211.1999   clare-rod12@email.com

RANDGOLD FOOD COMPANY – Charlotte, North Carolina (*continued from prior page*)

- **Provided compensation due diligence** on two key acquisitions. Helped merge the new businesses (together valued at $1.5 billion in sales) into Randgold's compensation system and provided training on compensation strategy to new leadership teams, their managers and their employees
- **Authored the "Compensation Guidelines" policy booklet** for management on compensation issues which included: objectives, merit increases, transfers, promotions, demotions, salary ranges, job evaluation, exemption status, and various other guidelines. Available online and offline.

EQUINIX CORPORATION – Charlotte, North Carolina
Leading global insurance and financial services organization with revenues of $9 billion.

Manager – Compensation & Benefits   **(Year – Year)**
Senior Compensation Analyst   **(Year – Year)**
Compensation Analyst **(Year – Year)**
Promoted from senior analyst into this key managerial role accountable for designing and implementing a broad range of compensation, incentive and base salary initiatives for 3,500 employees. Key contributions in the above roles:

- **Chaired five regional task forces in re-evaluating the compensation** for 1,500 positions using a point factor plan and external benchmarking. 94% of recommendations approved by senior management.
- **Revised the sales incentive plan for 120 sales managers** worldwide. New plan contributed to more profitable sales and greater cross-selling based on executive feedback.
- **Developed of performance-based Incentive Plans** for 200 Sales and IT associates.
- **Coordinated year-end bonus and stock options** managed Employee Stock Purchase Plan and managed Salary Budgeting process & system using SRCPR software

EDUCATION & AFFILIATIONS

B.S. in FINANCE
Minor: Psychology
Chicago State University, Chicago, IL

Certified Compensation Professional (CCP) — [Year]
Currently pursuing Certified Benefits Professional (CBP) Certification

Professional Affiliations:
Detroit Area Compensation Council – Treasurer, Board of Directors [Year] and [Year]
WorldatWork – Membership Committee

Resume 15: *Change Agent That Delivers Bottom-Line Results*

MICHAEL S. McDOWELL, CBP
18201 N. Lake Street • Bradenton, FL 33232
(555) 461-9023• michael.s.mcdowell@gmail.com

SUMMARY

EMPLOYEE BENEFITS EXECUTIVE with significant experience managing comprehensive benefit programs for executive, exempt, non-exempt, unionized and non-union populations. Certified Benefits Professional (CBP) and change agent who has played a lead role in winning employee support for benefit plan changes delivering over $5.2 million in cost savings.

PROFESSIONAL HIGHLIGHTS

FLORIDA MUTUAL BANCORP, Bradenton, FL
Director – Benefits, Payroll & HRIS   *[Year] – Present*
Recruited to oversee benefits, payroll and HRIS for Florida's largest independently-owned bank with 8,200 employees in 18 locations. Ensured corporate compliance with federal regulations on health care and benefits. Managed a full-range of benefits programs, including health and wellness, 401(k), legacy pension, retiree medical, external benefit service providers, carriers and third-party administrator relationships and all open enrollment and employee communications programs.

- **Led effort to harmonize benefit programs** across all locations and align managed care programs with current health care legislation -- resulting in $2.4 million in annualized savings.

- **Drove initiative to provide individualized reports** to all employees to highlight value of their benefit package. Effort contributed a reduction in turnover from 11% to 4% and increased satisfaction with benefits by 5.8% on follow-up organization health surveys.

- **Identified and delivered $650,000 in annual savings** by changing actuarial services, which included outsourcing pension administration.

- **Increased 401(k) plan enrollments by 9.75%** through aggressive employee education efforts.

- **Reduced healthcare costs by $2.2 million** by adding two higher deductible plan options.

NATIONAL PACKAGING CORPORATION, Philadelphia, PA
Director – Employee Benefits, Corrugated Box Division *[Year] – [Year]*
Led the employee benefits function for the corporation's largest division -- supporting $1.2 billion in sales and 12,000 employees (80% unionized). Ensured benefits compliance with 12 union collective bargaining agreements and divisional compliance with ERISA, COBRA, FMLA laws.

- **Major contributor to 19 employee benefit changes** in all expiring union agreements saving $1.1 million in costs --working with HR, business leaders and health care providers.

- **Launched the first-ever self-service system** for employees for managing their HR and benefits – achieving an employee utilization rate of 90% the first year.

- **Improved compliance and cut costs by $150,000** by streamlining processes and outsourcing programs (COBRA, disability, pension plan administration).

-continued...

Resume 15: Page Two

MICHAEL S. McDOWELL, CBP
michael.s.mcdowell@gmail.com • (555) 461-9023

Manager –Employee Benefits, Corporate HQ *[Year] – [Year]*
Managed third-party administrators and benefits carriers which included cost control initiatives and performance guarantees. Served as subject matter expert for health & welfare escalated appeals and managed a team of 4 benefits administrators. Collaborated with legal counsel in order to develop benefits programs with particular focus on health care reform, compliance, improvement and cost containment.

- **Led the team which identified and executed $1.8 million** in annual company-wide benefit cost savings through plan design changes and bi-annual benefits audits.

- **Project managed the Open Enrollment training effort for 12,000 employees** in 14 divisions
  – including new changes in enrollment procedures health care plans (medical, dental, life/AD&D, vision and others).

- **Reduced corporate-wide workers compensation costs by 7%** over two years through closer partnering with site HR managers and more aggressive investigation, challenge and follow-up efforts.

Manager – Human Resources, Pittsburgh, PA *[Year] – [Year]*
Developed broad HR generalist skills providing support for this 800-employee unionized site. Coached managers on handling benefits, employee complaints and labor relations issues. Assisted with staffing exempt and non-exempt positions. Played a lead role on an integration team that designed and developed a new benefits plan for 3 business units.

- Served on a task force that restructured manufacturing operations and reduced 120 positions.

- Established a reputation as the #1 "go-to" resource for managers and employees on HR issues.

Senior Benefits Administrator, Corporate HQ *[Year] – [Year]*
Benefits Administrator, Corporate HQ *[Year] – [Year]*
Hired to act as liaison between employees and service providers and assist in problem resolution for the Company's 2nd largest division – supporting 4,000 employees. Advised and counseled management and employees on benefits. Served as main contact for employee benefits related inquires. Participated in the negotiation of renewals and explore competitive benefit options.

EDUCATION & LEADERSHIP AFFILIATIONS

B.S. in Business Administration, University of Pittsburgh
Won Eagle Award – Top Individual HR Award at National Packaging, [Year]

Certified Benefits Professional (CBP), World at Work
Vice President -- Florida Compensation & Benefits Association
Executive Board Member -- DuPage Workforce Board
Society of Human Resources Management

Resume 16: Out of Work, Doing Part-Time Consulting Projects

BLAIR LEE
812 River Road -- Nashville, TN 23222
blair.lee@gmail.com - (817) 467-9044

SUMMARY

HR Executive With 10+ Years of Labor Relations Experience.
Track record of implementing successful workforce solutions with positive P&L impact.
Proven ability to drive change in unionized, non-union, product and service-based companies.

EXPERIENCE

LEE EMPLOYEE RELATIONS CONSULTING, LLC
Founder & President [Year] - Present
Independent Consulting Company focused on employee relations issues with small and medium businesses. Currently provide assessments and solutions to companies which maximize the contributions of hourly workforces in their organizations.

Key projects:
- **Worked with the CEO & the senior leadership team of an oil company** to establish a new performance management program for hourly employees that contributed to the achievement of 117% of business plan for the current calendar year.
- **Served as Chief Negotiator** for a microchip technology firm in their contract negotiations with the Teamsters Union achieving 95% of management's negotiations objectives and business priorities.
- **Helped re-position a chocolate company as an "employer of choice"** in the local area for hard-to-find hourly talent, resulting in virtual elimination of all external search costs versus $300,000 in the prior year.

NATIONAL TRUCKING COMPANY, Cleveland, OH
Director – Employee Relations. [Y e a r] – [Y e a r]
Fifth largest trucking and transportation company in the U.S with 12,000 employees.
Recruited from Kraft to head Employee Relations for the Eastern Region – largest region in the company. Worked with key executives to develop and implement a highly effective "People Plan" that enabled the region to achieve its business, labor relations and talent objectives.

Key results:
- **Executed 26 salaried employee benefit changes saving $2.7 million in costs** --working with the corporate HR task force. This included pension changes, a revised pay-for-performance plan and an innovative on-the-spot bonus program to improve exempt employee engagement in the business.
- **Negotiated two early union contract settlements** with the United Steelworkers Union. Both contracts were within budget, done without a work stoppage and included work rules changes which lowered manufacturing costs by $1.2 million annually.
- **Increased diversity hiring representation from 38% to 56%.** Implemented a Minority Internship Program – increasing participants from 3 to 24.
- **Introduced weekly scorecards** in every business unit and tracked results which increased employee engagement in the business from 40% to 75%.

-continued-

Resume 16: Page Two

BLAIR LEE – Page 2
blair.lee@gmail.com - (817) 467-9044

KRAFT GENERAL FOODS, Buena Park, CA
3rd largest food company in the United States with 60,000 employees.

Senior Manager –Employee Relations, Buena Park, CA   [Year] – [Year]
HR leader for the newly acquired Global Juices Company with $250 million in sales and 1400 employees. Brought in to help integrate this business into the Kraft system. Reported directly to the General Manager, Global Juices and SVP-Human Resources.

Key results:
- **Drove changes in corporate culture,** countering "status quo" mindset to fuel business improvement initiatives that optimized efficiencies and enhance employee productivity.
- **Developed & led the Global Foods' first-ever formal succession planning process** and "room" review approved by the CEO and Board of Directors.
- **Cut HR expenses by $250,000** by establishing business-wide HR metrics and leading detailed staff assessments.

Manager – Employee & Community Relations, Nashville, TN   [Year] – [Year]
Promoted to head the HR function for this 1600-employee, unionized site as a key member of the leadership team.

- **Championed the acquisition and retention of key talent.** Improved retention of key people by 17% over prior year's total through individualized development and mentoring for our 12 highest potential managers. Attracted 5 high quality outside hires to upgrade senior management positions at the site.
- **Contributed to a 12% reduction in grievances,** a 9% improvement in employee engagement survey results through the introduction of a new management-union collaborative labor relations model.

Manager – Employee & Community Relations, Hersey, PA   [Year] – [Year]
Led the HR function for this 500-employee site as a key member of the leadership team.

- **Maintained non-union status** by defeating a Teamster union organizing campaign which maintained manufacturing flexibility and avoided $2.4 million in SG&A costs.
- **Improved employee engagement in the business by 12%** though executing enhanced training and development programs, utilization of employee task forces, and enhanced communications initiatives.

Manager – Safety & Health, Hersey, PA   [Year] – [Year]
Brought in as the first safety manager for this five-year old manufacturing plant with 500 employees.

- **Introduced accident prevention programs** and provided safety training that improved the company's lost time frequency rate by 42% and days lost due to injury by 58%.
- **Implemented safety and return-to-work programs** that recovered more than $800,000 in worker's compensation premium costs.

EDUCATION & AWARDS

Bachelor of Science –Occupational Health & Safety, Indiana State University
"Top 50 Asians in Business" recognized by *Asian Business Today*– [Year]

Resume 17: Summary Conveys His Story Quickly

Oliver Jameson, SPHR 11870 Alp Drive, Johns, IL 64022 | ojameson@yahoo.com | 377.515.4513

Summary

Drives Improved Business Results Through Optimizing Talent and Building High-Engagement Cultures

SENIOR HUMAN RESOURCES EXECUTIVE & TRUSTED BUSINESS PARTNER. Proven track record in crafting strategies that optimize talent and build high-performing cultures that support double-digit revenue growth. Adapt at collaborating with senior leadership teams, forging consensus and engaging the workforce in implementing high-impact HR strategies.

- Growing & Retaining Talent
- Building Workforce Capability
- Innovative Compensation Programs
- Change Management & Transformation
- Succession Planning & Development
- Merger & Acquisition Restructuring
- Field & Corporate Collaboration
- Employee Relations
- Trusted Advice & Counsel

Business Experience

CROMAX GLOBAL SYSTEMS, Rosemont, IL
Global technology firm with revenues of $7.2 billion worldwide and 22,000 employees around the globe.

Vice President, Human Resources (Year – Present)
Key member of the Cromax Americas Field Leadership Team and HR Leader for corporate headquarters with dual reporting to the President, Cromax Americas Division and SVP, Global HR. Leading a team of 23 HR professionals.

- **Developed talent acquisition strategies** that allowed Cromax to average of 7% sales growth in the last three years with 20% fewer locations, 12% fewer employees while delivering improved revenues per location/employee.
- **Helped improve revenue/employee by 6%** by capturing merger and acquisition synergies using effective organization design and change management strategies.
- **Oversaw $85 million annual G&A budget** which funds talent management activities for US and European sites.
- **Led the implementation of corporate guiding principles** identified by senior leadership that transformed an indifferent workforce into a high-performance workforce that delivered more revenues for the firm and more income for themselves.

Senior Director, Human Resources (Year – Year)

- **Reduced staff by 9.7%** over the last year to maintain profitability & continue to generate double digit sales growth.
- **Piloted a new sales talent acquisition business model**, which increased product sales/employee by 38%.
- **Managed the HR function's expansion into Europe**, which now has 70 offices and 5000 employees.
- **Led function centralization and captured HR synergies** during two mergers in last three years.
- **Successfully defended $10.5M in total EEO charges** by partnering with outside counsel to in multiple US locations.

MONARCH GAMING, Las Vegas, NV
Fortune 300 gaming company that provides products to 2000 hotels and resorts globally.

Director of Human Resources (Year – Year)
Led HR function supporting 550 employees with two HR generalists. Chief HR Business Partner supporting the Sales & Marketing SVP and the leadership team.

- **Developed a new sales commission structure** with the compensation team that rewarded for firm-wide sales into major accounts. Results contributed to a 14% revenue growth improvement.
- **Streamlined talent management and leadership development processes** across sales and marketing teams in 14 field sales offices on the West Coast.

-continued-

140

Resume 17: Page Two

Oliver Jameson, SPHR – Page 2 | 377.515.4513 | ojameson@yahoo.com

---

Director of Human Resources - continued
- **Travelled to all regional offices with senior leadership** to connect with employees to developing a desirable place to work based on positive employee engagement survey results.
- **Assimilated 11 acquired firms** into the culture, business and performance process in various locations.

JOHNSON PRODUCTS COMPANY, Chicago, IL
North American based manufacturer of beauty and cosmetic products with $900 million in revenues.

Human Resources Manager (Year – Year)
Served as the HR Business Partner to the EVP of Sales and sales senior sales organization.
- **Improved retention of high performing sales staff by 12%** by partnering with sales managers on an initiative to "re-recruit" at-risk candidates.
- **Implemented an accelerated high-potential, leadership development program** that helped identify top talent to senior leadership and ensured these leaders were "promotion-ready" within 18 months.
- **Participated in the HR Taskforce that developed a new HR call center** in Chicago Heights, IL to support 300 US employees. This was the first shared services center for staff on HR inquiries, benefits and payroll.
- **Co-facilitated annual talent review and succession planning sessions** with the executive team and crafted tools and development assignments to revitalize the high-potential sales leader program.
- **Advised on change management** initiatives for transitioning 500-employees from suburbs to downtown Chicago.

*Recruitment & Staffing Supervisor (*Year – Year)
Sourced, recruited and interviewed candidates for salaried, technical and hourly positions.
- **Achieved a 17% increase in minority engineering talent** by partnering and building relationships with key feeder colleges and universities.
- **Under tight budgetary constraints, met annual cost per hire objectives** and recruitment goals of 20-30 high-potential IT, R&D and engineering positions per year.
- **Introduced the first-ever formal new employee orientation program** for all supervisor, manager and executive-level employees with 92% positive feedback from participants.

NIPPON STEEL COMPANY, East Chicago, IN
World's 6th largest fully-integrated steel manufacturer with 6,500 employees.

Sr. Human Resources Analyst (Year-Year)
Human Resources Analyst (Year-Year)
Production Supervisor (Year – Year)
Moved from line position as production supervisor accountable for 120 hourly employees to staff role in HR. Promoted from HR analyst to senior analyst in one year. In HR, interviewed job candidates, handled employee relations issues and conducted new employee orientation for a client base of 1,400 employees.

--- **Education & Professional Development** ---

Advanced Management Program in Human Resource Management -- University Of Michigan, Ann Arbor, MI

SPHR (Certified Senior Professional in Human Resources) -- Society of Human Resources Management

B.S. Industrial Engineering -- Purdue University, West Lafayette, IN

Resume 18: A Bold, Full-Design Resume

MARIAN CLARK-SMITH, MBA, SPHR

12252 Sycamore Avenue, Sacramento, CA 31444
418-871-3707 - mariancsmith@gmail.com

SUMMARY

HUMAN CAPITAL LEADER AND STRATEGIST with verifiable record of delivering Human Resources and business results for health care organizations in the following areas:

▪ HRIS Creation/Implementation	▪ Staff Retention/Development	▪ Six Sigma Implementation
▪ Employee/Labor Relations	▪ Change Management	▪ Regulatory Compliance
▪ Talent Management	▪ Health Care Staffing	▪ Performance Management

EXPERIENCE

Executive Director - Human Resources, Huntington Health Care ▪ *[Year] - Present*
Provides human resources and executive leadership to a $350 million healthcare organization with 7 hospital and service locations and approximately 3,200 employees. Develops and execute corporate HR systems, manages all workplace issues and collaborates with executive leadership on developing talent.

- **Reduced HR service response time by 35%** and improved employee morale and satisfaction levels by 80% after launching "Above & Beyond Employee Service" initiatives.
- **Attained and maintained 99% placement rate** for all key positions nationally.
- **Lowered annual turnover rate** for physicians and specialists from 12% to 4% - best in the industry.
- **Developed and implemented the organization's HRIS system** at $157,000 below budget.

Director - HR & Chief Administrative Officer, Lake Forest Heath Care ▪ *[Year] – [Year]*
Led $260MM healthcare administrative organization providing community medical services through six locations. Planned and directed healthcare operations, human resources and change management initiatives. Consulted on multi-level operations and implemented policies/procedures that improved services and profitability within the organization's Healthcare Delivery System.

- **Contributed to $4MM in operational cost savings** through the elimination of non-value added work, consolidation of jobs and utilizing external service providers.
- **Improved medical staff readiness from 38% to 88%** effectiveness -- using advanced scheduling procedures and lean Six Sigma Strategies.
- **HR change leader in the merger of 4 healthcare organizations** supporting $100MM in revenue.
- Refurbished over 130 emergency medical support vehicles, producing $6.5MM in realized cost savings.

Director – Human Resource Services, National Health Services Corp ▪ *[Year] – [Year]*
Directed HR management and administrative work processes for 4,500 employees geographically dispersed in 12 locations across the US.

- **Increased average engagement** among nurses and support staff from 75% to 92% across all sites.
- **Lowered annual turnover rate** for nurses from 18% to 9%.
- **Produced 18 consecutive months of operations** with a 100% accuracy, timeliness, and satisfaction rating.

-continued-

Resume 18: Page Two

MARIAN CLARK-SMITH, MBA, SPHR

Page 2 -- 418-871-3707 - mariancsmith@gmail.com

EXPERIENCE (CONT'D)

Director – Human Resources & Administration, General Micro-Devices ▪ *[Year] – [Year]*
For three years, led the Human Resources, Purchasing, Safety and Payroll groups for this $90 million manufacturer of specialty computer devices with 600+ employees – before the business closed in *[Month, Year]*. Reported directly to the CEO.

- **Proactively utilized unique low-cost, high-value recruiting techniques** which staffed the organization quickly and saved the organization thousands of dollars in search fees.
- **Oversaw monthly performance appraisal process** for 100+ employees.
- **Implemented comprehensive safety programs** resulting in a company-record 400 days without a lost-time accident and $800,000 savings in worker's compensation costs.
- **Successfully resolved 32 audits/complaints** in the company's favor with the EEOC, OFCCP, DOL, SPBR, SERB and the civil courts.

During the business downsizing and closure process:
- **Led HR in supporting 3 phased reductions-in-force** to support the efficient closure of the business. Used early separations, retention agreements, position consolidations, attrition and schedule changes to minimize impact on sales, customer service and employee morale.
- **Executed the employee transition process** by providing severance packages, in-house outplacement support and career counseling for all 600+ employees. 74% of all separated employees landed new positions within six months.

Additional Human Resources Experience --Nekoosa Packing Company
- Employee Relations Manager *[Year] – [Year]*
- Training & Development Supervisor *[Year] – [Year]*
- Labor Relations Trainee *[Year] – [Year]*

EDUCATION & TRAINING

Masters in Business Administration (MBA), University of Texas
Bachelors in Health Care Studies (BA), University of Texas, Magna Cum Laude (3.8 GPA)

Certified Senior Professional in Human Resources (SPHR)
Certified Black Belt in Six Sigma
Lean Six Sigma, Executive Strategy Program – Purdue University
Executive Healthcare Recruiting Certification – University of Rhode Island
Senior HR Executive Development Program – University of Michigan

RECOGNITION & AWARDS

Winner of SHRM California HR Professional Excellence Award *[Year]*
Member of National SHRM Health Care Panel *[Year] – [Year]*
Human Resources Certification Institute (HRCI) Panel Expert

Resume 19: HR Leader with Military Training

JIM SAMUELS

345 N. Price Avenue #3602
Blue Gardens, LA 34554
(555) 555-5555 jim_samuels345@email.com

SUMMARY

HR LEADER WITH SIX YEARS OF BUSINESS EXPERIENCE. A military trained, strong achiever with a bias for action and proven quantifiable results. Bilingual in Spanish.

Areas of expertise include:

Recruiting & Staffing	Leadership Development
Compensation/Incentive Programs	Total Rewards/HR Business Planning
Performance Management	Employee Development
Talent Retention	Labor Relations/Union Avoidance
Change Management	M & A HR Due Diligence & Integration

PROFESSIONAL EXPERIENCE

WESTERN NATURAL GAS SERVICES, New Orleans, LA
Third largest U.S. natural gas operation with $35 billion in revenues and 35,000 employees.

Sr. Regional Manager - Human Resources [Year] - Present
Currently leading the XYZ Region HR team which supports 12 geographically diverse sites and 1,100 employees. Major priorities include talent management, employee relations, union avoidance strategies, M&A support and rightsizing. Managing an HR staff of six.

- Designed and implemented a special incentive plan to engage and reward salaried and hourly employees for cost management ideas. Plan to date has delivered $1.7 million in previously unidentified savings.

- Executed the HR due diligence activities involving the purchase of two natural gas plants valued at $1.2 billion and involving 1,200 employees.

- Led two successful union avoidance campaigns with Electrical Workers Union in Atlanta, Seattle without a disruption in the business.

- Led succession planning & leadership development programs which improved retention of key talent in Marketing & Sales by 25% over prior year's total.

- Reduced customer service headcount by 10% through leadership of voluntary separation program.

Manager - Human Resources [Year] – [Year]
Managed full range of HR programs and services for 400 employees at four regulated and two non regulated natural gas units supporting $1.2 billion in revenue.

- Recognized by the CEO for leading the #1 recruiting, diversity and college relations initiative in the Company. Improved representation of women and Latinos in key positions by 25% in one year.

- Managed the divestiture transition activities of 52 salaried and hourly employees in a $25 million natural gas plant.
  --Led exit activities, severance arrangements and counseling for all impacted employees.
  --Retained the top performing 10%, placing them in other roles within the business.

- Drove the proactive employee relations strategy – successfully avoiding two organizing attempts by the IBEW and UFCW.

-continued-

144

Resume 19: Page Two

JIM SAMUELS – Page 2

(555) 555-5555   jim_samuels345@email.com

PROFESSIONAL EXPERIENCE - continued

Manager – Recruiting & Talent Acquisition [Year] – [Year]
Promoted to manage all phases of the recruitment and talent acquisition process for the Corporate Finance and IT organizations. Accountabilities included requisition entry, interview scheduling, offer letters, pre-employment process, new hire set-up, new hire orientation & candidate experience.

- Led a team of 6 short-term contractors which filled 100-125 positions annually on time and within budget.
- Improved offer acceptances for IT candidates from 52% to 77% through improved candidate visits and better positioning of the opportunity.

Staffing Specialist [Year] – [Year]
Joined company to provide recruiting and staffing support for 500 managers and employees in the corporate office. Assisted with the selection and placement of exempt and non-exempt positions.

MILITARY – U.S. NAVAL OFFICER

- **Regional Admissions Director**, U.S. Naval Academy, Annapolis, MD.

- **Pilot/Department Head**, VP 5, NAS Louisville, KY, Patrol Squadron Mission Commander.

- **Shipboard Division Officer**, U.S.S. Garnett (DLG 5) Newport, RI; Officer of the Deck Underway.

- **Reserve Naval Officer:** continued USNA admissions and P 3 flight duties until retirement in [Year].

EDUCATION

- **MA, Human Resources Management**, UNIVERSITY OF SOUTH FLORIDA

- **BS, Engineering**, U.S. NAVAL ACADEMY

- **Advanced Program in Human Resources**, LOYOLA BUSINESS SCHOOL

PROFESSIONAL AFFILIATIONS

- Society for Human Resource Management

- U.S. Naval Academy Alumni Association

- Southeast Human Resources Group - Executive Committee & Chair

OF NOTE

- Bilingual in Spanish

- Past Class President, U.S. Naval Academy

Resume 20: *Highlighting Global Experience*

EMILY W. ARRINGTON
17009 W. Holiday Street • St. Louis, MO 58143
(402) 891-1654 • e_arrington@gmail.com

SUMMARY

GLOBAL SENIOR HUMAN RESOURCES EXECUTIVE, THOUGHT LEADER AND BUSINESS ADVISOR.
Extensive experience acquiring & optimizing talent internationally (Europe, Africa, Asia Pacific, Mexico).
Proven track record delivering measureable HR results in global manufacturing firms.

EXPERIENCE

HYDRAULIX, INC., St. Louis, MO -- *$10 billion global manufacturer of premium hydraulic equipment,*

Vice President, Human Resources - International   [Year] – Present
Leading worldwide organization of 15 Global Region HR Directors and staff of 75 HR professionals located in Europe, Africa, Asia Pacific, Mexico and Canada. Reporting directly to the EVP, Global Operations and SVP of HR. Providing full HR support for the 22,000 international employees for largest business unit in the company.

- **Developed first-ever Global People Plan** to rapidly acquire talent needed to support the massive international growth of the company. Results so far:
  --Filled 100% of all open Global EVP/SVP/VP roles, some of which had been vacant more than a year.
  --Filled the top 675 "profit-generating" positions – cutting recruiting time-to-fill from 112 to 49 days/hire.
  --Reduced cost per hire by 32% through innovative talent attraction strategies.
  --Attained 92% client satisfaction rate with quality of new hires.

- **Upgraded and re-aligned the performance management system** for all salaried personnel around the globe. Results contributed to the International division achieving 122% and 135% of business plan – following five years of performance ranging from 80-95% of plan.

- **Led complete reorganization of all key functions** reporting to senior leadership teams in Europe, Africa &Asia Pacific. Eliminated 2 reporting levels and redundant services valued at $5.7 million annually.

- **Executed a Global Diversity and Inclusion strategy** for 22,000 employees worldwide which improved our employee engagement index by 12.7% after one year and won the "President's Award for Excellence."

BAIDCOM PRODUCTS, INC., Chicago, IL -- *$1.2 billion privately-held manufacturer of automotive products.*

Senior Vice President & Chief Talent Officer   [Year] – [Year]
Reported directly to CEO. Led the company's global human resources strategy with additional accountability for labor relations and corporate communications. Supported 4,500 employees, 20 manufacturing sites, 10 sales offices and 30 distribution centers worldwide.

- **Developed the talent strategy to support the acquisition of two new businesses** with sales totaling $210 million. Did HR due diligence, developed compensation/retention/exit packages and developed communication plan resulting in smooth integration of these businesses into the parent company.

- **Championed the 22.5% improvement in employee engagement results** across all sites and sales offices through targeted leadership development, aggressive communications, positive employee relations and specific follow-up actions.

- **Led the redesign of group health plans**, stressing wellness, managed healthcare and cost containment --- which reduced annual healthcare costs by over 13%.

- **Collaborated with executive leadership to revamp the sales recruiting, training and incentive programs.** Results increased revenue per salesperson from $250,000 to $333,000 in 14 months.

-continued-

Resume 20: Page Two

EMILY W. ARRINGTON
Page 2 • (402) 891-1654 • e_arrington@gmail.com

Vice President -- Employee Relations   [Year] – [Year]
Growth position with responsibility for employee/labor relations, recruitment/hiring and industrial safety for 3,000+ employees across 20 manufacturing sites.

- **As management's Chief Labor Spokesman, re-negotiated 12 labor agreements** representing all hourly employees which improved manufacturing schedule flexibility by 22% and other contract enhancements valued at $6.2 million.

- **Led the defeat of 2 union organizing attempts** (Teamsters, IBEW) which avoided a potential 8% increase in labor costs.

- **Led the reduction in on site OSHA safety violations by 22% across all sites** by implementing a full-slate of OSHA-approved safety-compliant programs, rigorous protocols and procedures.

- **Oversaw successful completion of numerous undercover security operations** which led to the arrest and prosecution of individuals involved with drug use and/or theft.

MOTOROLA, Schaumburg, IL - *Global leader in wireless communications with $80 billion in revenues and 60,000 employees worldwide.*

Director - Corporate Staffing   [Year] – [Year]
Position created to meet increased staffing demands of on organization which doubled in employee head count during a three-year period. Led all company staffing activities including supervision of 15 internal and external recruiters.

- **Staffed 300-person national sales force** for Automotive Division -- 4 months ahead of schedule.

- **Staffed entire 28-person Emerging Markets Organization** (HQ and field) to support International expansion.

- **Led the staffing for skilled and unskilled positions** in manufacturing operations to enable company to move from a one to a three shift operation and capture manufacturing efficiency improvements of 33%.

EDUCATION

Master of Science, Human Resources Management
Golden Gate University, San Francisco, California

Bachelor of Science, Business Management
Calumet College, Whiting, Indiana

PROFESSIONAL LEADERSHIP & DEVELOPMENT

American Management Association – Regional 12 President [Year – Year]
Human Resources Executive Program – University of Michigan
Change Management Leadership – NTL Institute
Michigan State University -- Advanced Labor Negotiations
Cornell University -- Interest-Based Bargaining

The Story & Strategy Behind These 20 Example HR Resumes

Resume 1: *HR Leader With a Specialty.* <u>The strategy:</u> Kaminski's resume is targeting a very specific HR role. He's looking to work with Sales organizations and teams. Note how this is described in his Summary, through his use of keywords, his accomplishments and speaking experience.

Resume 2: One Page HR VP Resume. <u>The strategy:</u> Silverstone has many versions of her resume. In this shorter, one page version (which she provides at networking events), she captures her executive experience succinctly by emphasizing her last two roles – which are most relevant to the role she's seeking.

Resume 3: Recent Grad Seeking First Full-Time Position in HR. <u>The strategy:</u> Washington uses the one page format preferred by new college grads. She uses the limited space well by playing up her graduate degree, strong intern experience and campus leadership activities. Her GPA is just okay, so she doesn't include it all.

Resume 4: Light on HR Experience, Applying for Posted Job. <u>The strategy:</u> Martinez customized this resume for a specific, posted position at Citibank. Frankly, she lacked much of the experience required for position – so she used executive endorsements to offset this and emphasized her two-language fluency as a differentiator to land the job.

Resume 5: Employed in 3 Companies in 4 Years. <u>The strategy:</u> Cooper moved through 3 companies in 4 years. Her Apple job only lasted 3 months. While this isn't extreme job hopping behavior, she wants to limit any potential negative perceptions by focusing the resume primarily on her current job.

Resume 6: Using the CAR (Challenge, Action, Result) Approach. The strategy: Fredricks employs the CAR approach because it clearly illustrates his long-term history for taking on challenges and delivering HR results. Visually, this style is unique and comes across compellingly.

Resume 7: Outstanding HR Experience, But No Degree. The strategy: Bates' biggest liability is that she has no degree. She does not hide it, but offsets it well by highlighting her PHR certification, HR results, glowing CEO testimonials and her professional affiliations.

Resume 8: HR Professional With Line Management Experience. The strategy: McFee's resume positions her HR and P&L experience as her towering strengths. She also uses keywords in her Summary and 3 summary boxes to bring attention to her most significant contributions.

Resume 9: Customizing Resume For A Specific HR Job. The strategy: This resume has been customized by: (1) capturing the exact job title from the job description at the top of the resume (2) using bulleted keywords in the Summary taken directly from the job description and (3) matching the resume's key contributions to those highlighted in the job description.

Resume 10: Recognized For HR Excellence. The strategy: Doren's resume includes her HR-related awards and recognition both inside and outside of her organization as well as her high GPA. This is not the time for modesty.

Resume 11: Targeting a Specific Geographic Area (California). The strategy: Bucker loves California (CA), has no desire to relocate. Has designed his resume to attract CA firms – stressing his PHR-CA certification, state familiarity, expertise in regulations and legal mandates specific to the state.

Resume 12: BEFORE Version - Functional Resume. The strategy: Jones uses a functional resume to divert attention away from her job hopping and towards her accomplishments. However, this tactic is obvious to most savvy recruiters. For this reason and others provided in Chapter 1, functional resumes are NOT recommended.

Resume 12: AFTER Version – Reverse Chronological Resume. The strategy: This AFTER version uses the more accepted resume format. It's lessens the appearance of job hopping by combining her short-term jobs together under one title "Director–Human Resources." This conventional presentation of her qualifications has a better chance of landing interviews.

Resume 13: Universal Resume Highlighting Important Keywords. The strategy: Blakely's universal, full-design resume features nine "searchable" keywords he's identified as most relevant for his targeted job. He highlights them in his Summary and throughout his resume. He'll convert this resume into a LinkedIn profile and post it on other online job sites.

Resume 14: Accentuating Board & Comp Committee Experience. The strategy: Rodriguez is seeking a senior role in C&B. She stresses s her experience in working with Boards of Directors and Comp Committees, which is a key differentiator and critical to landing the top job she seeks.

Resume 15: Change Agent That Delivers Bottom-Line Results. The strategy: McDowell's resume is selling his ability to lead and drive employee benefit changes and reduced costs with minimal disruptions to the workforce – a highly desirable skill. Note the words used to convey this.

Resume 16: Out of Work, Doing Part-Time Consulting Projects. The strategy: Lee has been out of work for 20 months and has done independent, part-time consulting work while searching for her next corporate job. Note how she has positioned this experience citing specific results.

Resume 17: Summary Conveys His Story Quickly. <u>The strategy:</u> Jameson creatively uses his Summary to display his most important experiences combined with keywords so that they can be viewed at a glance – and tell his story in just a few seconds.

Resume 18: A Bold, Full-Design Resume. <u>The strategy:</u> HR resumes don't have to be boring. Clark-Smith uses this bold resume template to draw attention to this printed, full-design version of her resume. Note also the use of keywords in her Summary and her effective deployment of impact statements throughout.

Resume 19: HR Leader with Military Training. <u>The strategy:</u> To supplement his HR experience, Samuels includes and stresses his military naval officer training and bilingual skills. He also effectively uses keywords in his Summary.

Resume 20: Highlighting Global Experience. <u>The strategy:</u> HR professionals with global experience are in high demand at all levels. Note how Arrington has positioned and accentuated her significant international experience.

12

7 FREE HR RESUME TEMPLATES YOU CAN DOWNLOAD & USE RIGHT NOW!

As a bonus for purchasing this book and to accelerate your pursuit of HR interviews, I've provided some free resume templates to make your resume creation efforts a little easier.

Even with the guidelines provided in this book, designing and formatting a resume sucks! It can eat up a lot of your time attempting to get spacing, margins and formatting right. And frankly, that's time better spent focusing on your resume's content while networking and contacting employers.

So I thought I'd save you hours of angst by putting together SEVEN resume templates that you're free to use to give you a running start. You can download all seven of them here:

> **HRResumeSecrets.com/documents2-1168807.htm**

These templates give you a fast start no matter what kind of HR role you're pursuing. All seven are slightly different, so pick the one which makes the most sense for you. Also be mindful of using certain designs and color. In most cases, a simple, uncomplicated, black and white document will suffice.

13

CONQUERING THE MOST COMMON HR RESUME PROBLEMS & DILEMMAS

This chapter will run through how to solve many of the most common resume problems and dilemmas so that you highlight your good points, while downplaying the not-so-good ones.

So without further ado, let's get to it...

Resume Dilemma #1:
LENGTHY PERIODS OF UNEMPLOYMENT OR HUGE TIME GAPS BETWEEN JOBS

If any of these apply to you, and they are mishandled on your resume, most recruiters won't wait to ask you about them in person -- they'll simply trash your resume.

Here are five options for addressing these issues:

Option 1: Describe Yourself as a "Consultant"

This is a common way for executives to cover job gaps. But, candidly, when recruiters see "Consultant" on a resume, most of them automatically think it's just a fancy way of saying you have been out of work. So, if you're truly going to list yourself as having been an HR consultant, you absolutely must have specific human resources projects and results on your resume. I'd even recommend having in your hip pocket the names and phone numbers of people who can verify the work you did.

For a "Consulting" example: Check out Blair Lee's resume in Chapter 11. Before landing her current role, she had been out of work for 20 months and did independent, part-time consulting projects during this span -- while she searched for a full-time corporate gig. Note how she treated this time period on her resume as just another job...and how she was able to cite specific consulting deliverables and results. This is an excellent example to follow.

Option 2: Highlight "Volunteer" Work

If you didn't consult, did you do any volunteering? Depending on the nature of the experience, you can count that as work experience on your resume. Again, list it just as you would list your other jobs -- with job title, company name, job description, and dates of employment. Below is an example:

Volunteer Fundraiser, Make A Wish Foundation
French Lick, IN, *[Month, Year] to [Month, Year]*
- Recruited and trained 14 volunteer fundraisers.
- Planned and promoted 3 successful fundraising events including an auction, dinner and concert which generated over $125,000 in pledges.
- Increased contributions by 25% over the previous campaign.
- Received "Gold Key Achievement Award" for leadership.

Option 3: Cite Your Role as a "Parent" or "Student"

If you can't come up with a title that's relevant then pick one that accurately describes your role and shows you have good character (such as "parent" or "student"). Consider everything you were doing during that time (such as travel, volunteer work, internships, training or family projects) and if possible, present them so they're relevant to your job search objective. For example, a person who cared for an ill parent for two years and is now looking for a way back in the job market might write:

> **Primary Home Care Provider for terminally ill relative.**
> *[Month, Year]* - *Present.*

Here are other related "job titles" successfully utilized by HR professionals to cover gaps:
- Full-time Student Pursuing Executive MBA
- Independent Research Project on Workplace Trends
- Full-time Parent
- Family Management
- Family Financial Management (or Estate Management)

Special Note: Raising a family is an entirely legitimate reason to have a gap, so don't try to hide or embellish by using silly titles like Household or Domestic Engineer. You just need to help an employer understand the reasons you were out of the workforce. Your challenge will be demonstrating that your skills are fresh. So, in citing that you were caring for your family, also be sure to include any temporary work or volunteer jobs you did with the school and in the community. You'll want to showcase that you've remained active, engaged and sharp.

Option 4: Use Years, Not Months for Your Work History
There is no rule that says that you need to list every single month/year when listing dates on your resume. This is especially true if you've been in one role over a year or if your position spans multiple years. For example, you could say 2011-2013 (rather than May, 2011-March, 2013) which would give you some room to cover the gaps.

Using just years achieves two things: (a) it makes it easier for the reader to quickly ballpark the length of time you stayed at each job and (b) it conceals gaps that happened within a span of two calendar years.

Here's an example:

Director, Human Resources Operations, XYZ Company
(2011 – 2013)
Sr. Manager - Compensation & Benefits, ABC Corporation *(2008 -2011)*

In the above, it doesn't specifically say which month these years occurred, which miminizes the appearance of a gap. In fact, listing all the months on your resume can be an unnecessary detail (although some recruiters, especially executive recruiters, may still insist on months being listed).

Option 5: Omit a Job (or Two)
You don't need to include all your experience on your resume, especially if you have been in the workforce for years. It's acceptable to limit the years of experience you include on your resume to 15 years when seeking a managerial or professional position and ten years if you're seeking a position in a rapidly growing high-tech organization.

Most Importantly, In Deciding Which of These Five Options
To Use – DON'T LIE On Your Resume and Be Prepared
To Address These Gaps Candidly In The Interview!

The above suggestions are designed to help you get interviews without fabricating your employment history. Research shows that less than half of recruiters notice gaps during their initial sift through resumes anyway. This means that half do and will no doubt ask outright about any gaps in your employment history. When this happens: TELL THE TRUTH! Most employers verify work history and if you put incorrect information on your resume, I can guarantee that they'll find out.

Explaining a gap in employment during an interview can be tricky. The best approach is usually to address the issue in a direct and forthright manner. Provide a clear rationale for taking time off if the break was voluntary. If you took time off to deal with a particular issue like caring for a sick relative or completing coursework and are ready to return to full time employment, make it clear that the reason for your hiatus has passed.

If you were laid off due to a work force reduction, it will be important to provide any evidence of strong performance as you explain the circumstances surrounding the downsizing. Whenever possible get recommendations from supervisors, colleagues and clients confirming your competence.

Of course, it will be more difficult to make a strong case if you were fired due to performance issues. If you are now targeting a job which requires different skills or competencies then you might emphasize how your strengths are better suited for the job at hand. If you've taken action to correct any problems which led to your dismissal then you should mention the steps that you've taken. Also, avoid any negative characterization of your former employer since many prospective employers would take your former company's side.

Finally, Avoid Making a Big Deal Out of Resume Gaps

Lots of HR folks have less-than-perfect work histories, so don't worry if you do too. What's key is that you present your past so the employer either doesn't notice or feels okay about your work record.

Make sure your resume emphasizes the positive by stressing the constructive activities you've engaged in during your gap period such as consulting, volunteer work, workshops or coursework, consulting or free lance work. And, exude enthusiasm for returning to work and make a very strong case for why your target job would be exciting for you and an excellent fit.

Resume Dilemma #2:
TOO MANY JOBS

Leaving one job for a better one can be a smart career move. But too many job changes in a short time span can give hiring authorities cause for concern.

If you fall in this camp, the best solution is to **consolidate your jobs.** The example below was excerpted from the Thea Jones resume in Chapter 11. Thea had three jobs in 21 months. She consolidated all three jobs into one span of time—and then combined the contributions from all three jobs as follows:

DIRECTOR – HUMAN RESOURCES [Year – Year]
Eastern Illinois University – Charleston, IL
Cleveland School District – Cleveland, OH
Gary City Schools – Gary, IN

- **Chief spokesperson in negotiations with largest teacher's union in Ohio.** Achieved inflationary caps on healthcare, multi-tier wage schedules, consolidated multiple schedules and improved work rules – with a work stoppage.
- **Implemented profile tools to predict teacher success and improve retention**, expanded mentoring program through grants resulting in improved performance, and enhanced the effectiveness of background investigations and record-keeping.
- **Successfully managed audits/complaints** with EEOC, OFCCP, DOL, SPBR, SERB, Civil Service, civil courts.
- **Identified/problem-solved a $21M underfunding situation** without impacting current budget, preventing greater cuts.
- **Implemented value-based health plans**, wellness programs, eligibility audits, facilitated labor/management committees.
- **Identified illegal practice between a broker and carrier** resulting in awards to the employer, license suspensions for offenders, and changes in state legislation regarding transparency and broker compensation.
- **Designed and implemented various key compensation programs** -- skill-based programs, performance-based compensation, traditional and executive compensation programs.

Keep in mind that in using this format, you're *still* going to be questioned about the number of jobs in such a short period of time. But presenting them as a "consolidated package" is more likely to produce interviews for you.

It doesn't seem to matter to employers that the average job in the U.S. only lasts two and a half to three years, or that companies expand and contract more these days than they ever have in the past. The implication is that employees should be more stable *than the companies that they work for.* (How ironic!)

How much job hopping is too much? In a Robert Half survey, HR executives interviewed said that an average of six job changes in 10 years or three job changes in two years can prompt worries you're a job hopper. In these cases, there's a natural assumption on the part of the hiring authority that you're going to be at your next job for only one year or less. They worry that you either get fired too often, you easily get bored or you just can't seem to pick the right job for you.

And that's a red flag because the last thing an employer wants is to hire you and have to replace you twelve months later.

Here are some additional tips on putting a positive spin on your resume if you've been job hopping:

Turn Attention Away From Your Employment Dates
Avoid putting employment dates in prominent places, or making them bold, or including them in the headings or anything else that will bring the reader's eye to it. Try putting the dates at the end of the description of your jobs. You can also avoid using months and include just years. Some recruiters and HR people will insist on the exact dates, some won't.

Combine All Short Term Assignments Into One Group
Lump any short term, interim, contract, freelance jobs together in one entry on your resume. You can use a collective header such as "Consulting Projects" in which you list all your short term assignments to date. The aim of your resume is to demonstrate your skills and experience for a specific organization and job. It's not a document listing all the tiny events that have occurred in your life.

Omit Anything Irrelevant On Your Resume

Again, there's no rule saying you have to include all jobs you ever did on your resume. You decide what goes on there. This isn't your autobiography.

When Contacted, Be Open About Your Job History

Be prepared for questions. If you left a job for legitimate reasons such as cutbacks or mergers, say it. This is often out of your control and happens frequently in today's volatile economy. One acceptable reason for job hopping could be that you were exploring different jobs to see what you were meant to do – and now you absolutely know that the job you're applying for is perfect.

Write A Great Cover Letter

Make sure you write a fantastic cover letter that will stand out (to outweigh the resume). This cover letter must indicate your knowledge of the company you are applying for as well as how you're going to add value to your prospective new employer.

The bottom line: Your real aim here is to take focus away from you being perceived as a high risk hire. By emphasizing your contributions and experience as opposed to what is missing, you can minimize coming across as a job jumper.

Resume Dilemma #3:
RECENTLY DEMOTED

Getting demoted can be problematic when preparing your resume. Below is an example of how to handle this type of challenging situation:

EXAMPLE: Carole Demoted Six Months Ago.

The following *Before* example is an excerpt from a resume Carole had been using—without success. Carole, a VP of HR, was demoted in a corporate merger between the ABC and XYZ companies. On her resume, she wanted to position herself for other VP HR positions like the one she had for two years. But, her move to a Director position from an HR VP role, in the same company, will likely raise performance concerns in a hiring manager's or recruiter's mind.

Here's the excerpt from her BEFORE Resume...

PROFESSIONAL EXPERIENCE

ABC CORPORATION / XYZ, INC.
Director - Compensation & Benefits *(Current)*
Re-assigned to integrate all company-wide compensation and benefit programs for the XYZ's North American businesses.

Vice President, Human Resources *(2 years)*
Led HR function supported 8,500 employees in a 7-state area for a business generating $970 million in revenue. Attracted, developed and retained talent in sales, marketing and operations. Managed 11 HR directors and an indirect staff of 25 admins.

Achievements:
- Collaborated with senior management to reposition the division as an "employer of choice." Strategy cut key position turnover by 9%and improved executive offer acceptances by 27% in one year.
- Led the creation of *ABC University* which provided online leadership training for 3,500 employees at all levels with a 94% utilization rate.

To further mask the perception that Carole was demoted, she also used this closing paragraph in her cover letter:

I have successfully led HR for the number-one branch in the nation for the past several years. With the company merger and the reorganization of HR, my responsibilities have been shifted to New York City. Rather than relocate, I have requested a comp & benefits position to remain in the Chicago area (my husband and I are long-time residents). Given my management track record, I am taking this opportunity to explore HR leadership opportunities such as the one with your firm.

Unfortunately, these approaches did NOT work for her. So, here's what she did to her resume that **generated more interviews:**

Her AFTER version...

PROFESSIONAL EXPERIENCE

ABC CORPORATION / XYZ, INC. *(Year – Present)*

HUMAN RESOURCES LEADERSHIP EXPERIENCE:
Rapidly promoted through three key HR roles with ABC Corporation. As vice-president HR (2 years), supported 8,500 employees in a 7-state area for a business generating $970 million in revenue. Managed 11 HR directors and indirectly responsible for a staff of 25. As compensation & benefits director, with the acquisition by XYZ, earlier this year, chartered to integrate all company-wide compensation and benefit programs for the XYZ's North American businesses.

Vice President - Human Resources
Achievements - ABC CORPORATION:
- *Developed HR Strategy:* Collaborated with senior management to reposition the division as an "employer of choice." Strategy cut key position turnover by 9%and improved executive offer acceptances by 27% in one year.
- *Enhanced Leadership Capability:* Led the creation of *ABC University* which provided online leadership training for 3,500 employees at all levels with a 94% utilization rate.

Compensation & Benefits Director
Achievements - XYZ, INC.:
- *Revised Pension Designs:* Headed project team which redesigned current pension plan to comply with changed ERISA guidelines. Projected savings: $11.2 million.
- *Led Health Care Program Improvements:* Gained approval for the consolidation of multiple PPO's into one national offering saving $6.3 million in annual costs.

Here's a breakdown of the changes she made:

- Titled the narrative paragraph as "Human Resources Leadership Experience" and began the description by referencing her prior promotions.
- Elaborated on her accountabilities while Vice President.
- De-emphasized the present position as Director, by placing it after the VP role.
- Because she had spent a year in the Director position, she added accomplishments to further demonstrate her consistent history of strong performance.
- To help readers follow what she accomplished in each position, she listed the word *Achievements* followed by the name of the company (ABC Corp. or XYZ, Inc.).
- Dates for each job have also been dropped – replaced by one date covering her entire tenure with the organization.
- With all these changes, she no longer needed a long explanation in a cover letter that could be misinterpreted.

NOTE: Everything in this example is 100% truthful. The big change is that her most important experience has been highlighted, elevated and positioned in the best possible light. Once she's landed the interview, she can then tell her whole story.

Resume Dilemma #4:
OVERQUALIFIED FOR THE JOB

Sometimes you might find yourself in a situation where you are compelled to apply for position requiring less responsibility or experience than you already have.

Let's say you've just got laid off your job as VP of HR for a $3 billion dollar firm that went bankrupt. You live in a rural community of 50,000 people (where the company HQ was located) and you absolutely don't want to relocate or travel. You and your family enjoy the schools and lifestyle. In this situation, it doesn't matter how much experience you've had because you've restricted yourself geographically. No one can do anything about the availability—or, should I say, lack of available VP HR jobs in the community you've limited yourself to.

So, in a case like this, it's best to have at least a couple of different resumes:

- *One resume* that's "full-blown" and reflects every bit of HR leadership you've shown and every accomplishment that you ever achieved.
- And a *second resume* that might downplay the extent of your leadership experience and focuses instead on the major HR projects you've worked on.

Obviously, only you can judge whether this is a viable strategy or not. Often, in small communities or economically disadvantaged job markets, the job you want may not be available. Certainly, you can broaden your search geographically to expand possibilities. But if you don't want to, it may make sense to be an *employed* HR professional rather than an *unemployed* HR Vice President.

Resume Dilemma #5
DEALING WITH DISCRIMINATION & BIAS

In putting together your resume it's important that you write it so that it deals with potential bias relative to your...

- Ethnicity
- Gender
- Sexual preference
- Marital status
- Age
- Health
- Weight
- Height
- Beauty
- Perceived social class
- Address
- Attire
- Political and religious beliefs
- Education
- Physical disability

Bias, you say? Discrimination? In HR? C'mon, let's be real with each other. While the majority of HR professionals are women and there is strong track record of diversity in the HR profession, the business news headlines still indicate that discrimination is alive and well in pockets in many workplaces. And yes, even in HR.

Strategies for dealing with this are very complex and personal. One approach is to not reveal any information that will prejudice your chances of getting an interview. To some, I know, this can be extremely insulting. They are justifiably proud of themselves and perceive that concealing facts as playing up to the bigots. This is perfectly understandable, and that is where personal choice comes in. To that end, here's my advice:

- **Omit references to your health, physical characteristics, age, and marital status.** All are irrelevant to most, if not all HR jobs. However, recognize that most hiring authorities will look you up on LinkedIn and will draw conclusions based on your picture, school dates, hobbies, ethnic affiliations and any other personal or family information you include as part of your profile.

- **Some potential sources of bias can't be hidden, so don't try...instead, turn them into assets.** If you have a Spanish-sounding surname such as Ruiz, and you have mentioned that you are bilingual and speak fluent Spanish, you will be clearly assumed to at least be of Hispanic descent. So play up your bilingual abilities as an asset.

- **If you've achieved certain major recognition awards (e.g. *"Top 50 Asians in Business," "Top 40 Under 40 in the Midwest,"* etc.) definitely include them on your resume.** Don't conceal these. These are the types of rare achievements that you should justifiably be proud of and, though they are revealing, you'll certainly want to promote them without hesitation.

Here's the acid test: If you really want to include any of the preceding information and are worried about the impact it may have, it probably means you would not be happy working for the organization in question in the first place. It's also worth remembering that, just because the person who reads your resume may be biased, this doesn't mean the people you will work with or for are too.

Again, don't shoot the messenger here! Use your own judgment. Just remember that you don't want to be eliminated from an interview simply by what's on your resume, when you can easily avoid it.

Resume Dilemma #6
HANLDING AGEISM

Age presents a special challenge. Believe it, or not, some HR job seekers are reporting age bias and discrimination beginning as early as the mid-thirties. And by the time you reach your mid-forties, you can be considered washed up in some HR departments or by some hiring authorities (though don't expect anyone to tell you this directly).

If you believe this is an issue, preparing a resume that emphasizes your value (not your age) is a good first step in your job search. Here are eight ways to age-proof your resume:

#1: Be careful how far back in your job history you go. You don't have to start with your first job if it's not to your advantage. As long as everything on your resume is true, it's fine to leave out something (such as older years of employment).

This is a big mistake job seekers make. Like I've mentioned before, if it's more than 15 years old, employers generally don't care. Hiring managers are most interested in "what have you done for me lately" and "what can you do for me now." So concentrate primarily on your recent career. If you feel compelled to delve into earlier experiences, create a section called "Early Career" and provide just the highlights and no dates.

#2: Watch your language. Avoid age-revealing statements such as "35 years of experience" or age-defining clichés such as "seasoned professional."

#3: Show that you're current with technology and industry trends. Are you an expert at using employee involvement groups, HR re-engineering or using MySpace in recruiting? While these initiatives and programs were once cutting-edge, they're out of date now and have been replaced with new HR initiatives and technology. Show that you've kept up with the times by removing antiquated programs and initiatives and highlight your knowledge of modern, state-of-the-art HR practices.

#4: Drop dates of education. This is a tough call, because hiring managers who want to know a person's age will go right to the "Education" section and do the math. If your education occurred 20-25 years ago, it's probably to your advantage to drop the dates.

#5: Keep your school names updated. If you graduated from a school that has since changed its name, include the new name. If you are concerned about discrepancies in case an employer asks to see a transcript, write the former name of the school in parentheses.

#6: Show that you've been continually learning or taking on new roles. The key is to demonstrate that your skills are fresh and in demand. It is important that you show that you are flexible and willing to adapt to organizational changes.

#7: Quantify and expand on your achievements. As a professional with a long work history, this is your chance to accentuate the positive. You have what younger HR professionals may lack — years of practical experience. Provide examples of how your performance contributed to your employers' goals, mission, and bottom-line results.

#8: Whenever possible, use names of companies that still exist or use their new name. An example of this is replacing Nippon Steel (the current name) for Inland Steel Company (the former name).

The goal is to have the executives who are reading your resume focus on your accomplishments and what you bring to the party. You don't want them to get hung up on your age.

Resume Dilemma #6
RELOCATION TO A DIFFERENT CITY

In pursuing any non-executive HR job requiring that you move away from your current location, you will find many employers not eager to foot the full bill for your relocation. If that's the case, here are some recommendations:

- **Be prepared to pay for your own relocation.** Because of the housing market (especially in large cities), many firms have cut back dramatically on their relocation budgets for many new hires. You may be able to negotiate this once you have an offer, but don't bank on it.

- **If you live far away from the job you're applying for, take your physical address off the resume.** Use just your email address and phone number. Some companies only interview local candidates to avoid expensive relocations. While your cell phone number's area code can be revealing too, it's often less so because of the variety of area codes given out by phone companies.

- **Don't tell a prospective employer *before* you've interviewed that you are not in the area.** Eventually you're going to have to explain to a hiring manager that you don't live in the area and that you need to relocate. But it's wise to do this *after* you've had a chance to sell yourself in the interview.

In short, I'm not suggesting you deceive prospective employers. I'm just telling you to remove all potential barriers to getting interviewed. Concerns about relocation on the part of a prospective employer shouldn't be a bigger problem than if you were fired from your last three jobs or if your references are awful. Location may wind up being a deal killer, but you don't want the issue to keep you from getting the interview.

Resume Dilemma #7
OBSCURE TITLES

I touched on this briefly before, but thought it deserved a bit more attention. Here's the deal: Some HR titles can be confusing, especially to General Managers, COOs, CEOs and even to hiring authorities within the HR profession. If you currently reside in an obscure title that does not convey the level of your responsibility, on your resume add a parenthetical statement that gives the reader clarity and a better frame of reference.

For instance:

HR Business Partner - Global New Products, XYZ Inc. *(Equivalent to Senior Director HR - New Products. Reported directly to GM, New Products)*

Senior HR Integration Leader – New Acquisitions, ABC Inc. *(Equivalent to Corporate VP HR, reported directly to company COO).*

Or these examples, which list more conventional HR titles first, followed by actual titles in parentheses.

Director, Human Resources - Sales *(HR Business Partner)*

Director, HR Data Systems *(HR Data Optimization Lead)*

Both of these translations will add clarity to your resume and will also improve your chances of being found in keyword searches of resume databases.

We've now concluded our discussion of resumes. Let's now move on to cover letters and their role in supplementing your resume.

14

THE LITTLE KNOWN SECRET
ABOUT USING COVER LETTERS
& THE ONLY ONES YOU'LL EVER NEED

The little-known secret about cover letters is that they are no-where near as important as a lot of job search experts will tell you. In fact, the truth is...

**Most cover letters are read only when the hiring authority
has <u>already</u> <u>read</u> your resume and wants to know
more about you.**

Remember, since your resume is going to get scanned in fifteen seconds or less, you can assume that your cover letter isn't going to get much more attention and probably a lot less.

However, there is a solution. The best way to increase your chances of it getting read is to:

- Send it <u>directly</u> to the hiring authority by name.
- Make it short and to the point (especially if you send it electronically).
- Design it so that it makes an impact FAST with specifics that scream: "You need to interview me!"

It will also help if you:

- List your accomplishments that apply to the specific job opening.
- Use bullet points to attract attention.
- Make sure it's personally signed (with an electronic signature, if necessary).
- Always have a postscript (P.S.) that is an "action item" (it will get read before the body of the letter does).

So, avoid full-page cover letters! They will rarely, if ever, get read.

Also, skip the "Dear Sir" intro. Find out exactly who is behind the open position. Sites such as LinkedIn or Zoominfo.com are great resources finding the names of company insiders. In addition, you might be able to call the company and ask who the hiring manager is for the open position, or use your network to learn the names of managers at the company. If you can't find out the name, *"Dear Hiring Manager"* is most appropriate. Skip, *"To Whom it May Concern"*— it won't concern anyone!

Remember, you are trying to sell the potential employer on the idea of granting you a face-to-face interview, not on hiring you. Even if your cover letter gives all the reasons you ought to be hired, you're going to have to get interviewed anyway. So, it's important to sell yourself only one step at a time—in this case, your cover letter *and* your resume should work in combination to help you secure the interview.

With that in mind, here are four sample cover letters you can adapt for your own use – and are the only ones you'll need.

Cover Letter #1:
THE IDEAL COVER LETTER

If possible, have a personal phone conversation with the hiring authority first. And then send your resume with this brief cover letter to act as a reminder. In this situation, you've established rapport and your letter and resume has the highest likely of getting read. A typical cover letter of this type should look something like this:

Dear _____,

Thank you for the time we spent on the phone. Based on what we discussed, I would be an excellent candidate for the position of

_____.

Attached is my resume. You stated you were looking for someone who:
- *Was an HR Director with 10 years of experience in the gaming industry.*
- *Has managed a staff of at least 5 HR generalists.*
- *Has experience with maintaining union-free status in manufacturing settings.*
- *Has a clear track record of making difficult decisions*

As you can see from my resume:
- *I've been an HR Director and have 12 years of experience in the gaming industry*
- *I have managed as many as 4 HR generalists; overall, there was a staff of 12 people*
- *I've had 3 years experience as the HR leader maintaining union-free status at 2 different manufacturing facilities.*
- *I have a clear track record of making difficult decisions, especially with my last firm. We had to close 4 locations and lay off 175 people in order to maintain profitability.*

Sincerely,

Jane Smart
Email: j_smart68@yahoo.com
Phone: 312- 667-8888

P.S. I will call you tomorrow at 1:30 p.m. about meeting with you this week.

It's that simple. Don't make your cover letter any more complicated or longer than this sample. Use three or four short bullet points with as many quantifiable statements as possible. Then ask for an appointment

Cover Letter #2:
THE PAIN LETTER

The term "pain letter" has been popularized by Liz Ryan, CEO & Founder of the Human Workplace (HumanWorkplace.com). Pain letters get your credentials into the hands of hiring authorities for jobs not posted or that may not even exist yet! The idea here is to go directly to the hiring manager with your cover letter and resume that speaks directly to him or her regarding a "pain" you absolutely know that exists in their department or organization.

Here is a sample Pain Letter:

Rodney Smithson, VP Human Resources
Green Mountain Coffee
412 Brewster Avenue
Baylor, CA 32567

Dear Rodney,

I was fortunate enough to catch your presentation at the Baylor Talent Management Conference two weeks ago, and was delighted to hear you discuss Green Mountain's plans for diversifying the business to capture the rapidly growing segments in emerging markets. Clearly, your products have definitely hit a chord with the coffee-loving public here in the U.S. and the global expansion plans you mentioned are quite exciting.

You also mentioned that Green Mountain's number one challenge is recruiting and retaining sales professionals to support your growth plans. As HR Director for U.S. National Sales for Liquid Tea Products, I led a team of HR professionals supporting a $1 billion sales organization. We accomplished the following:

- *Increased revenue per salesperson by 10% by utilizing an innovative sales assessment and development model that can be customized to any organization including Green Mountain's.*
- *Improved retention of high performing sales staff by 12% by partnering by initiating 3 key initiatives to "re-recruit" at-risk candidates.*
- *Enhanced sales capability through the creation of a "Sales Leadership Institute" that accelerated internal best practice sharing & imported external "best-in-class" sales practices.*

All of these initiatives could easily be adapted to the Green Mountain organization. If you have time for a telephone call or email correspondence to see where we might have an intersection of interests, I'd be delighted to learn more about your challenges and discuss how my experience might help.

Best Regards,

Jane Smart
j_smart68@yahoo.com
312-667-8888

P.S. In the meantime, I've attached my resume which might trigger other ways that could enhance Green Mountain's recruitment and retention of sales talent.

Notice how this letter addresses the key pain point. In situations like this, even if your pain letter hits that decision-maker's desk when there's no job, it could be the reason that they actually open up a requisition to hire someone. It's not that unusual for the manager to walk down the hall to the CHRO's or HR VP's office and say: "You know, you and I have been going back and forth and back and forth on whether we can afford another HR director. Look at this resumé. Look at this person who is writing to us about our stuff, what's going on with us. She's totally on the ball. Let's just bring her in here and see if she's a fit."

When that happens, then you're the only person that interviews for that job. And this happens every day. You don't have to wait for a job posting. It's just a question of whether they have budget to create a position.

COVER LETTER #3:
THE GENERIC APPROACH

If you don't have the luxury of a phone conversation beforehand or don't have a "pain" point to address, you might use the information you gathered from a job posting or plain old common sense and direct your letter to the decision-maker, generic-style. And your letter might look something like this:

Dear _____,

I understand you are searching for a proactive Human Resources Generalist for the home products division of your organization. Attached is my resume. As you can see:

- *I was selected by Corporate Global HR to lead a 5-person project team on flexible work arrangements which improved retention annually by 3 percentage points and saved $3.2 million in recruitment costs.*
- *I've contributed to a 12% reduction in the number of employee complaints filed and led 7 improvements in the company's job posting process.*
- *I started out on the ground floor as an HR analyst, then moved into compensation and benefits, then moved back*

into human resources management over a period of 8 years.

- *I offer stability. I've had only 2 employers in those 8 years.*
- *The owners of my previous firm will testify that they were able to successfully sell the organization to the new owners because of my HR leadership in the merger.*

Sincerely,

Jane Smart
j_smart68@yahoo.com
312-222-5551

P.S.: I will call you tomorrow at 1:30 for an appointment to meet in person.

P.P.S.: Enclosed [or attached] are the results of my 360 results our company did on all of its managers. You can see that I scored in the upper 5% of all managers surveyed globally.

Again, this letter is brief and too the point. Also, remember that it never hurts to include *numbers, stats* or *percentages* in your cover letter. Any quantitative fact that says "I'm good!" helps you get interviewed.

Cover Letter #4
REFERRAL LETTER

It's always best to actually *telephone* a personal referral or someone you have something in common with *before* sending your cover letter and resume to that person.

But if for some reason you can't, or you've left a number of messages with no call back, you can write a cover letter to accompany your resume. It would go something like this:

Dear _____,

A mutual friend of ours, Amanda Brixey, recommended that I forward you my resume. She said you and I have a lot in common, particularly when it comes to the University of Chicago Alumni Association.

I would like to meet with you to explore Human Resources opportunities either with you and your company or any others that you might know of. Mandy said you were the kind of guy I should get to know.

My resume is attached. I will call you tomorrow morning to see if there might be a convenient time that we can meet.

Sincerely,

Jane Smart
312-222-5551

It is important to begin the first paragraph with something personal. Remember, *don't focus on your needs!* Saying anything that implies, "I need a job," doesn't cut it. Hiring authorities care only about getting what they want. Now, if you can get what you want at the same time, things might work out for both of you. So, to insert a personal note, begin the first paragraph with something you might have in common, such as:

> *We both graduated from Purdue . . .*
> *We were both members of Alpha Phi Alpha. . .*
> *We both worked at XYZ Software Company . . .*
> *We both know . . .*

SECRETS OF GREAT COVER LETTERS

#1: Use the decision-maker's name. Again, let me reiterate, e-mailed (or snail mailed) cover letters and resumes sent to anyone other than the hiring authority feeling the "pain" won't get read.

All four of these examples are most effective when sent directly to hiring authorities. If a third-party screener reviews your resume (and a hundred others) you won't get a response unless you an absolutely perfect match (which is highly unlikely).

If you're targeting the SVP or EVP of Human Resources, the odds are good that you'll find that person on the company's website. However, if you're looking for someone a bit farther down the food chain, that may be tougher. To help you locate the name of the contact that could well be your next boss, here are three resources you can consult:

- Conduct a LinkedIn search on the company's name and your target person's most likely title.
- Use ZoomInfo.com to find the manager you're looking for.
- Google the company name plus the title — 'your' manager's name may pop up in a search result.

It's easy to find a mailing address for a manager or executive, once you've got a name. If you check LinkedIn and your three-dimensional network and can't find a conduit person (someone who knows this person, who'd be willing to make an introduction for you). And if you can't locate an email address, then your best bet is to send a snail mail letter straight to the decision-maker's desk.

#2: Ask for the interview. There is the one thing you can say in a cover letter that will dramatically increase your chances of accomplishing its purpose...and that is *to ask the employer for the interview.* I've read statistics that have indicated job seekers who ASK for the interview in their cover letters are twice as likely to GET the interview. To accomplish this, below are several examples that you can modify and use.

Example A
I'm excited about the Director of Talent Acquisition position with XYZ Widgets and would love the opportunity to meet in person to further discuss my experience and the value I can offer

you as your next Director of Talent Acquisition. Please call me at 555.555.5555 to schedule an interview at your earliest convenience.

Example B
I would love a personal interview at your earliest convenience to further discuss my credentials with you. I can be reached at 555.555.5555 and will follow up as well to make sure you've received my information.

Example C
Thank you for your time reviewing my resume. I welcome the opportunity to discuss in a personal interview my qualifications and fit for the position. Feel free to reach me at 555.555.5555 at your earliest convenience.

Example D
Thank you for your time and consideration. I will follow up in one week to schedule a day and time we can meet to further discuss the position and my experience. You may also reach me at 555.555.5555 to schedule an interview.

Use any wording you're comfortable with. The key thing to remember is to close your cover letter by MAKING THE ASK.

#3: Don't Repeat Everything In Your Resume
Even though you've put a lot of effort into your resume, resist the urge to repeat all that great information in your cover letter. You'll grab more interest by briefly restating your main points. I recommend adding only your most relevant qualities and contributions, keeping it to a maximum of 4-5 bullet points. To guide you, try answering the classic "Why should we hire you?" question, and you'll be able to state your case much more succinctly

#4: Ensure Your Resume & Cover Letter Work Together.
First of all, the fonts should match. As insignificant an issue as this may seem, hiring authorities notice if your resume is written

in a mix of Georgia and Arial—and your cover letter is written in Courier New. Although this difference isn't necessarily going to be a deal breaker, it is something that could stand out to an anal manager who is looking for consistency between documents (in order to determine how serious you are about attention to detail). So, to be on the safe side, take time to ensure that your cover letter font matches the predominant font in your resume.

Secondly, information on both documents should match. The last thing you want is for a hiring manager to read about jobs or experiences in your cover letter you don't mention in your resume. This is why it's important that you take time to create a new cover letter with each resume so all of the information matches and is tailored to the position for which you are applying. The information in one should always match the other. If it doesn't, it will look as though you hastily threw together documents to submit—which is an impression you definitely don't want to give.

And thirdly, use the same high quality paper. If you're applying for a job the traditional way—by submitting a resume and cover letter on paper—it's important to make sure both documents are printed on the same high-quality paper. Again, consistency is important when applying for a job, and there's nothing more obviously inconsistent than turning in two documents printed on different types of paper.

Sometimes it's hard to imagine how many of the "little things" matter when applying for a job. Making sure a cover letter and resume match is high on that list and should be taken seriously.

HANDLING REQUESTS FOR SALARY INFORMATION WHEN SUBMITTING YOUR RESUME

Job postings or ads often ask that you send a resume, cover letter, and salary history.

I strongly suggest that you avoid providing a salary history when responding for a couple of important reasons: If your salary is higher than the position is paying, you may be screened out.

And, if your salary is lower, you may lock yourself into a lower salary than the company might have offered.

With that in mind, there are two approaches in managing salary requests.

Approach 1: Acknowledge the employer's request for salary and then sidestep any mention of past earnings with this sort of verbiage:

> *My recent earnings have been reflective of contributions made to my employer. I am confident your compensation plan is market-competitive, and I would be open to discussing this matter during the course of an interview.*

The downside to this strategy is that it could cause you to be screened out, never to be called for an interview. However, it's a chance you might want to take in order to keep your salary close to the vest. If you do, there IS a ray of hope. Typically, studies have shown that a candidate who looked very strong on paper yet averted the salary history request in most cases would still, at least, merit a telephone interview.

Approach 2: Acknowledge the employer's request and provide a salary range.

> *Regarding salary, my earnings as HR Director have ranged from $125,000 to $160,000 dependent on team-performance bonuses. Salary is not my primary motivation. Being part of a collaborative team that makes a difference in the company's results is.*

> *OR*

> *My past compensation has been in the mid-$125,000 - $160,000 range. My current requirements would be in line with industry standards.*

Providing a range is a happy medium between providing no information and providing your exact salary data. Here you're meeting the employer's needs half-way and provides a much better chance that your salary falls in the position's sweet spot.

In any event, avoid supplying a formal salary history on a separate sheet of paper with details of earnings history at each employer. Any of the sentences above, in most cases, knitted into your cover letter will usually suffice.

To recap, most cover letters are typically read after your resume, not before, and even then it's likely to only get a quick scan in many cases. Nevertheless, it important not to shortcut this step and use it as an opportunity to reinforce your resume and cement the reasons why you should be interviewed.

15

FINAL THOUGHTS

The goal of this book was to provide you with more than just a resume how-to book, but also provide strategies for marketing yourself and your credentials for the rest of your HR career. That said, before concluding, let me offer some closing thoughts:

You are the CEO and the number one marketer of your HR brand. As mentioned previously, you should consider yourself a "product" and your resume one of your marketing tools. Specifically, it's a 1-2 page ad for your brand that sells your contributions, skills and accomplishments so that you get your foot in the door for the kinds of interviews that can advance your career.

Your job search doesn't end when you find a new job. More than likely you'll be presented with this challenge again and again. For these reasons, keep your resume current so that you have it available quickly should you find yourself back in the job market, applying for an internal transfer or lobbying for a promotion.

A dynamite resume will give you confidence and demonstrate that you take yourself career seriously. It will also allow you to multiply your network by circulating it to your contacts to increase your chances of landing that dream HR job that could certainly be yours in the future.

Finally, in today's uncertain, volatile economy and with more people in the HR job market than ever before, you can't afford to come across as a commodity like everyone else. Instead, you need to stand out from your competition, be unique, highlight your special strengths and position yourself as someone who can deliver the kinds of results that employers want. And your resume – along with the advice in this book – can act as a catalyst for helping you do exactly that.

Onward!

Alan Collins

Alan Collins

CONNECT TO US ONLINE!
DISCOVER MORE WAYS TO SUCCEED IN HUMAN RESOUCES

Follow us on Twitter:
@SuccessInHR

Subscribe to our Blog:
SuccessInHR.com

"Like" us on Facebook:
Facebook.com/SuccessInHRDaily

Connect with us on LinkedIn:
http://LinkedIn.com/SuccessInHR

THE BRYAN A. COLLINS SCHOLARSHIP PROGRAM

The Bryan A. Collins Memorial Scholarship Program awards scholarship grants every year to minority students who demonstrate excellence in pursuit of their college degrees. Students selected for this scholarship must embody the values embraced by the late Bryan A. Collins -- great with people, great at academics and great in extra-curricular leadership activities.

Bryan Collins was a rising star and well-respected student leader at Tennessee State University. Bryan received his B.S. degree in Biology from TSU in May 2005. At the time of his passing, he was enrolled in the Masters program in physical therapy and anxiously looking forward to commencing his doctoral studies. On campus, he was a leader in the Kappa Alpha Psi fraternity, served on the Civic Committee, the Community Service Committee and help set strategic direction as a Board Member of the fraternity.

In addition, he found much success outside the classroom. He was voted Mr. Tennessee State first runner-up, was involved in the Student Union Board of Governors, was a founding member of the Generation of Educated Men and worked closely with the Tennessee State University dean of admissions and records.

Bryan found comfort and relaxation in sports, music, movies, video games, friends, good parties and just spending time with his family relaxing at home.

Key contributors to Bryan's scholarship program include the PepsiCo Foundation, the Motorola Foundation, Pamela Hewitt & Warren Lawson of Chicago and many other organizations and individuals. Additional details about Bryan, the scholarship program and how to contribute can be found at the scholarship website at: www.BryanCollinsScholarship.org.

ABOUT THE AUTHOR

Alan Collins is **Founder of Success in HR**, a company dedicated to empowering HR professionals and executives around the globe with insights and tools for enhancing their careers. He was formerly Vice President of Human Resources at PepsiCo where he led HR initiatives for their North American Quaker Oats, Gatorade and Tropicana businesses.

With 25 years as an HR executive and professional, Alan's corporate and operating human resources experience is extensive. He led an organization of 60 HR directors, managers and professionals spread across 21 different locations in North America, where he was accountable for their performance, careers and success. He and his team provided HR strategic and executional oversight for a workforce of over 7000 employees supporting $8 billion in sales. Alan also served as the HR M&A lead in integrating new acquisitions as well as divesting existing businesses; and he provided HR leadership for one of the largest change initiatives in the history of the Pepsi organization.

As the co-leader of the Quaker Tropicana Gatorade African American Network, Alan was selected as a member of the prestigious Executive Leadership Council, based in Washington D.C. He has also taught at various Chicago-area universities.

Alan is author of the *Unwritten HR Rules* and *Best Kept HR Secrets*. Both have been consistently ranked among Amazon's top 10 books for HR professionals. In addition, he has written over 100 articles and special reports on HR that have appeared in *HR Executive Magazine, HRM Today* and other nationally-known publications for human resources professionals.

He received his B.S. degree in Management and M.S. in Human Resources from Purdue. More about Alan and his works can be accessed at: www.SuccessInHR.com.

Made in the USA
San Bernardino, CA
09 December 2017